ON THE COVER
Fog flows through Cumberland Gap at dawn, viewed from the Pinnacle Overlook.

THIS PAGE
An idyllic setting at the Gap Creek Cascade provides a view of active stream dynamics in the park.

National Park Service photographs by Scott Teodorski (Cumberland Gap National Historical Park).

Cumberland Gap National Historical Park

Geologic Resources Inventory Report

Natural Resource Report NPS/NRSS/GRD/NRR—2011/458

National Park Service
Geologic Resources Division
PO Box 25287
Denver, CO 80225

September 2011

U.S. Department of the Interior
National Park Service
Natural Resource Stewardship and Science
Fort Collins, Colorado

The National Park Service, Natural Resource Stewardship and Science office in Fort Collins, Colorado publishes a range of reports that address natural resource topics of interest and applicability to a broad audience in the National Park Service and others in natural resource management, including scientists, conservation and environmental constituencies, and the public.

The Natural Resource Report Series is used to disseminate high-priority, current natural resource management information with managerial application. The series targets a general, diverse audience, and may contain NPS policy considerations or address sensitive issues of management applicability.

All manuscripts in the series receive the appropriate level of peer review to ensure that the information is scientifically credible, technically accurate, appropriately written for the intended audience, and designed and published in a professional manner. This report received informal peer review by subject-matter experts who were not directly involved in the collection, analysis, or reporting of the data.

Printed copies of this report are produced in a limited quantity and they are only available as long as the supply lasts. This report is available from the Geologic Resources Inventory website (http://www.nature.nps.gov/geology/inventory/gre_publications.cfm) and the Natural Resource Publications Management website (http://www.nature.nps.gov/publications/nrpm/).

Please cite this publication as:

Thornberry-Ehrlich, T. 2011. Cumberland Gap National Historical Park: geologic resources inventory report. Natural Resource Report NPS/NRSS/GRD/NRR—2011/458. National Park Service, Fort Collins, Colorado.

NPS 380/10577, September 2011

Contents

List of Figures

Executive Summary

This report accompanies the digital geologic map data for Cumberland Gap National Historical Park in Kentucky, Tennessee, and Virginia, produced by the Geologic Resources Division in collaboration with its partners. It contains information relevant to resource management and scientific research. This document incorporates preexisting geologic information and does not include new data or additional fieldwork.

Cumberland Gap National Historical Park preserves a geologic and landform feature that was a vital gateway to the west during the early expansion of the United States. The history of this area is intimately tied to the underlying geology and the geologic processes that shaped landforms such as Cumberland Gap. The gap is a deep notch across the otherwise continuous ridge of Cumberland Mountain. Additional geologic features, such as the White Rocks, guided early settlers moving westward on the Wilderness Road. It was a strategic outpost during the American Civil War, alternately occupied by Union and Confederate troops. The gap continues to be a valuable transportation corridor today.

Cumberland Gap sits on the far western edge of the Valley and Ridge physiographic province of the Appalachian Mountains. It is part of a regional geologic structure called the Pine Mountain thrust sheet created during the last major mountain building event of the Appalachians—the Alleghany Orogeny. Resistant sandstone ridges characterize the area. These ridges were shaped by processes that folded rock layers into the Middlesboro syncline to the west and the Powell Valley anticline to the east. Cumberland Gap is the primary geologic feature in the park. Its location is tied to an ancient fault—the Rocky Face Fault—formed prior to the last major Appalachian Mountain-building episode. Fractures and deformation associated with movement along this fault weathered the rocks. Over time, the weaker rock eroded away, forming a gap.

The geologic framework at Cumberland Gap forms the foundation for the ecosystem at the park. Geologic issues of significance for resource managers were identified at a Geologic Resources Inventory scoping meeting held in 2007. These issues include:

- Fluvial issues and pH changes in surface waters. Cumberland Gap National Historical Park contains the headwaters of several large streams, including Sugar Run, Martin's Fork, and Shillalah Creek, flowing downslope from the Cumberland Mountain ridgeline. Issues include riverbank and head-cutting erosion; the steepness of the stream courses causes instability along their channels with high-energy flow. Enigmatic decreases in surface water pH (to as low as 4.0) result in streams devoid of fish and other aquatic life. Acid rain, upland wetlands (organic decomposition), and pine tree soils may be contributing factors. The local geologic setting may also contribute to the low pH of certain streams. Sulfur-rich shales and coal beds exposed within a stream's watershed may result in chemical reactions between iron sulfide minerals and water may release sulfuric acid into the stream water, in a similar manner to acid mine drainage.
- Caves and karst issues. Chemical weathering of carbonate rocks (mainly limestone) occurs when naturally acidic groundwater reacts with soluble rock surfaces along subterranean cracks and fractures. Such dissolution forms a karst landscape. In the park, karst dissolution occurs in tilted, limestone-bearing rocks of Mississippian age (about 360 to 318 million years ago). Karst features include caves, conduits, sinking springs, pits, sinkholes, and springs. These types of features strongly influence how water flows through the subsurface. Studies using dye-tracing techniques can help delineate water recharge areas and flow paths. There are at least 30 named caves in the park. The cave resources at the park are generally not a target of emphasis and are understudied. Hazards associated with karst include sinkhole development and radon gas concentration. Radon naturally accumulates in the caves from the decay of uranium and thorium isotopes—both of which naturally occur in the Devonian-aged Chattanooga Shale (map unit MDc)(deposited about 375 million years ago). During the summer, cool air blows out of the lower opening of Gap Cave, circulating radon through the system.
- Mass wasting. The characteristically steep slopes of the park are prone to mass wasting events including landslides, block falls, slumps, and debris flows. Gravity, high precipitation events, frost heaving, root wedging, erosion, and karst dissolution are among the natural causes of mass wasting. Many slumps and slides occur within colluvial soils that mantle the base of slopes. Human activities such as landscaping, road construction, and facilities development may contribute to slope instability and even reactivation of old landslide features. Recent mass wasting in the park occurred where development destabilized the slope along the historic trace of Wilderness Road.

Other geologic issues discussed in the report are disturbed lands, Fern Lake watershed resource management issues, and seismicity.

Striking geologic features and processes are at not just at the park's namesake gap. Expansive and high quality rock exposures within the park have contributed greatly to understanding the geology of the area.

The park's rugged landscape is fashioned from rocks originally deposited in or near shallow seas. During Appalachian mountain-building approximately 300 million years ago, these rocks were folded, faulted, and shoved up and westward along the Pine Mountain thrust fault. Hundreds of millions of years of subsequent erosion beveled the ancient mountains, leaving behind limestones in Powell Valley, ridges of sandstone at Cumberland and Pine Mountains, and stream dissected upland areas near Middlesboro. The circular Middlesboro basin, adjacent to the park and easily visible from the Pinnacle Overlook, contains intensely deformed rock, evidence of an ancient meteorite impact.

Paleontological resources (fossils) in the park include marine organisms from ancient seas hundreds of millions of years old as well as much younger remains (tens of thousands of years old) found in caves.

This report also provides a glossary, which contains explanations of technical, geologic terms, including terms on the map unit properties table. Additionally, a geologic timescale shows the chronologic arrangement of major geologic events, with the oldest events and time units at the bottom and the youngest at the top. The timescale is organized using formally accepted geologic-time subdivisions and ages (fig. 23).

Acknowledgements

The Geologic Resources Inventory (GRI) is one of 12 inventories funded by the National Park Service Inventory and Monitoring Program. The GRI is administered by the Geologic Resources Division of the Natural Resource Stewardship and Science Directorate.

The Geologic Resources Division relies heavily on partnerships with institutions such as the U.S. Geological Survey, Colorado State University, state geologic surveys, local museums, and universities in developing GRI products.

Special thanks to: Martha Wiley (Cumberland Gap National Historical Park) for reviewing and providing comments on the "History of Cumberland Gap" section and Scott Teodorski (Cumberland Gap National Historical Park) for providing photographs used throughout the report. Dale Pate (NPS Geologic Resources Division and Carlsbad Caverns National Park) and Andrea Croskrey (NPS Geologic Resources Division) provided comments on the cave and karst section of the report.

Credits

Author

Trista Thornberry-Ehrlich (Colorado State University)

Review

Matt Crawford (Kentucky Geological Survey)
Steve Greb (Kentucky Geological Survey)
Jenny Beeler (Cumberland Gap National Historical Park)
Philip Reiker (NPS Geologic Resources Division)
Jason Kenworthy (NPS Geologic Resources Division)

Editing

Jeffrey Matthews (Write Science Right)

Digital Geologic Data Production

Heather Stanton (Colorado State University)
Philip Reiker (as a Colorado State University intern)
Georgia Hybels (NPS Geologic Resources Division)
Aaron Rice (Colorado State University intern)
Jeremy Hurshman (Colorado State University intern)
Dave Green (Colorado State University intern)
James Chappell (Colorado State University)
Ron Karpilo (Colorado State University)
Jason Isherwood (Colorado State University intern)
Cory Karpilo (Colorado State University intern)
Stephanie O'Meara (Colorado State University)

Digital Geologic Data Overview Layout Design

Philip Reiker (NPS Geologic Resources Division)

Introduction

The following section briefly describes the National Park Service Geologic Resources Inventory and the regional geologic setting of Cumberland Gap National Historical Park.

Purpose of the Geologic Resources Inventory

The Geologic Resources Inventory (GRI) is one of 12 inventories funded by the National Park Service (NPS) Inventory and Monitoring Program. The GRI, administered by the Geologic Resources Division of the Natural Resource Stewardship and Science Directorate, is designed to provide and enhance baseline information available to park managers. The GRI team relies heavily on partnerships with institutions such as the U.S. Geological Survey, Colorado State University, state geologic surveys, local museums, and universities in developing GRI products.

The goals of the GRI are to increase understanding of the geologic processes at work in parks and to provide sound geologic information for use in park decision making. Sound park stewardship requires an understanding of the natural resources and their role in the ecosystem. Park ecosystems are fundamentally shaped by geology. The compilation and use of natural resource information by park managers is called for in section 204 of the National Parks Omnibus Management Act of 1998 and in NPS-75, Natural Resources Inventory and Monitoring Guideline.

To realize these goals, the GRI team is systematically conducting a scoping meeting for each of the identified natural area parks and providing a park-specific digital geologic map and geologic report. These products support the stewardship of park resources and are designed for nongeoscientists. Scoping meetings bring together park staff and geologic experts to review available geologic maps and discuss specific geologic issues, features, and processes.

The GRI mapping team converts the geologic maps identified for park use at the scoping meeting into digital geologic data in accordance with their Geographic Information Systems (GIS) Data Model. These digital data sets bring an interactive dimension to traditional paper maps. The digital data sets provide geologic data for use in park GIS and facilitate the incorporation of geologic considerations into a wide range of resource management applications. The newest maps contain interactive help files. This geologic report assists park managers in the use of the map and provides an overview of park geology and geologic resource management issues.

For additional information regarding the content of this report and current GRI contact information please refer to the Geologic Resources Inventory website (http://www.nature.nps.gov/geology/inventory/).

Park Setting

With the significant exception of Cumberland Gap (fig. 1), Cumberland Mountain's crest is a virtually unbroken, 160-km-long (100-mi-long) ridge along the borders of Kentucky, Virginia, and Tennessee. Cumberland Mountain formed a historic barrier to westward colonial expansion. Daniel Boone explored the mountain pass as part of the Wilderness Road in 1775. Later, Cumberland Gap became a major thoroughfare across the Appalachian Mountains key to the settlement of the nation's interior. The gap was also a strategic military asset during the American Civil War.

Congress authorized Cumberland Gap National Historical Park on June 11, 1940. The park encompasses some 9,394 ha (23,214 ac) of Cumberland Mountain within Lee County, Virginia, Bell and Harlan counties, Kentucky, and Claiborne County, Tennessee (fig. 2). The park extends southwestward from White Rocks overlook along Cumberland Mountain across the gap and into the Little Yellow Creek watershed beyond Fern Lake Reservoir.

Cumberland Gap National Historical Park is just east of the boundary between two major geologic and physiographic provinces—the Appalachian Plateaus Province to the west and the Valley and Ridge Province to the east (fig. 3). Similar rocks are exposed in both provinces, however, pervasive deformation in the Valley and Ridge distinguishes them. Sharp cliffs, narrow ridges, notches, and steep valleys that characterize the landscape at Cumberland Gap National Historical Park result from weathering and erosion of geologic units, the structure of underlying geologic units, and differential weathering of these rocks (fig. 4).

Geologic Setting

The geologic framework at Cumberland Gap National Historical Park reflects the long history of Appalachian mountain building and weathering. The regional orientation of stratigraphic units, geologic structures, and faulting processes in the area controlled the formation and location of Cumberland Gap. Rich (1933) was one of the first geologists to provide a detailed description of the area's geology, including ideas about the development and evolution of the Pine Mountain thrust sheet (described below) that are still largely accepted today.

Cumberland Mountain is located between Pine Mountain and the Middlesboro syncline to the west and the Owen Valley anticline (called the Powell Valley anticline further north) to the east (fig. 4). These features are all part of the Pine Mountain thrust sheet, considered a classic example of a thrust sheet. Thrust sheets are typical of mountain-building events (called "orogenies") that formed the Appalachians (Dean 1989). The Pine Mountain thrust sheet is a large mass of rock with a thickness of about 1,200 m (4,000 ft) that was shoved westward between 3.2 to 21 km [2 to 13 mi] along a fault deep within the Earth's crust (fig. 5). The base of Pine Mountain, northwest of the park in Kentucky, illustrates the location of the thrust fault escarpment. Additional movement along smaller, localized faults (called "tear faults") resulted in further uplift and tilting of the originally horizontal, sedimentary-rock layers. Internal stresses within the Pine Mountain thrust sheet caused the formation of tear faults such as the Rocky Face Fault, which runs through what is now Cumberland Gap (fig. 5). Rock deformation associated with movement along the Rocky Face Fault created a zone of weakness in the bedrock. This weak zone then preferentially weathered in contrast to the rest of Cumberland Mountain forming the Gap, a 180 m-deep (600 ft) notch (Rich 1933). Smaller, narrower, and shallower gaps such as Butchers, Chadwell, and Gibson gaps are additional notches through the steep ridge of Cumberland Mountain.

A vast sedimentary rock record contained in the greater park area begins more than 500 million years ago in the lower Cambrian Period. These rocks are characterized by shale, siltstone, and sandstone, as well as carbonate rocks such as dolomite and limestone deposited in an open marine setting. Bedrock exposed in the park includes sedimentary rocks from the Devonian, Mississippian, and Pennsylvanian periods (between about 416 and 300 million years ago). The black Mississippian-Devonian Chattanooga Shale (geologic map unit MDc; see Map Unit Properties Table) is the oldest unit in the park and only appears in outcrop in the lowermost elevations. Deposited atop the Chattanooga Shale are mixed shales, cherts, limestones, and sandstones of the Mississippian Period including the Newman Limestone (map unit Mn), Fort Payne Chert (Mnf), Grainger Formation (Mg), and the Pennington Group (Mp). Dissolution of the Mississippian carbonate rocks formed caves such as Gap, Skylight, and Big Salt caves. Pennsylvanian-age units of the Breathitt Group form the majority of the rocks exposed within the park (see Map Unit Properties Table). Rocks assigned to the Breathitt Group include erosion-resistant sandstones that underlie the ridgetops and form steep cliffs. Pennsylvanian units also contain shale, siltstone, and numerous coal beds. More recent terrace gravels, landslide deposits and colluvium, and alluvial deposits mantle some of the bedrock within the park.

The town of Middlesboro, Kentucky, just west of Cumberland Gap National Historical Park, lies on an ancient meteorite impact structure and coincidentally, the Middlesboro syncline. A ring of faults surrounds the structure and the Paleozoic rocks within the ring are intensely brecciated, deformed, and susceptible to enhanced erosion. Rocks exposed at the surface today were once buried 300 m (1,000 ft) or more below the original crater (Thornberry-Ehrlich 2008).

History of Cumberland Gap

Cumberland Gap was used as a passage through Cumberland Mountain by migrating animals such as buffalo and deer for centuries. American Indian tribes such as the Shawnee and Cherokee, followed this game through the gap. Dr. Thomas Walker (a Virginia physician and surveyor) first mapped the location of Cumberland Gap in 1750 on behalf of the Loyal Land Company.

Early on, the gap proved to be a significant military asset. As part of the ancient Warrior's Path, it played a part in the on-going tensions between American Indian tribes, most notably the Cherokee and the Shawnee, as well as served as a trading route. The Treaty of Sycamore Shoals effectively ended hostilities in 1775, and the western frontier was opened to settlement and exploration.

That same year, the Transylvania Company and its representative Judge Richard Henderson of North Carolina hired Daniel Boone and 30 axmen to blaze a trail—later known as the Wilderness Road—from the Long Island of the Holston River (now Kingsport, Tennessee) to the Bluegrass region of Kentucky through the Cumberland Gap, a distance of more than 320 km (200 mi) (fig. 6).

By 1792, the year Kentucky became a state, more than 100,000 people had crossed Cumberland Gap, and in 1796, the road was widened to accommodate wagon travel. By the second decade of the 19th century, however, other routes, such as the Ohio River, became preferred routes west once the American Indian threat was removed, and traffic across the remote Cumberland Gap dwindled.

In the 1860s, the American Civil War renewed interest in the gap as a strategic feature. Confederate forces fortified the area in 1861 and abandoned it in 1862 upon the arrival of Union forces under General George Morgan. Union forces then occupied the area, constructing nine south-facing batteries. In September of 1862, they retreated and Confederates reoccupied the area. Union troops recaptured the area for a final time a year later. The fortifications were abandoned in 1866, leaving behind a landscape deforested by years of military activity (fig. 7).

The road fell into disrepair and earned the nickname of Devil's Highway because of the extreme difficulty wagons and horses encountered when crossing. Targeted as one of a very few roads in the nation to be macadamized for the automobile in the first decade of the 20th century, the road through the Gap soon became part of the famed Dixie Highway and flourished during the age of tourism in the 1920s and 1930s. Local efforts brought the significance of the Cumberland Gap to national attention, and in 1940 the Cumberland Gap National Historical Park was authorized by Congress.

Over the years, the road had been the scene of frequent accidents due to its steep and winding nature. One of the long range goals for the national park was the eventual restoration of the old Wilderness Road through the Gap. With the completion of the state-of-the-art twin-bore tunnel through the mountain in 1996, work on this dream was able to commence. Years of research, including the techniques of comparing historic photographs (fig. 7) with modern views to determine the exact location of the historic road, paid off when the restored Wilderness Road through the Cumberland Gap opened to the public as a walking trail in 2002.

Figure 1. View of Cumberland Mountain. The Mountain was a major barrier for the movement of people and goods—in this case for fog too. With the significant exception of Cumberland Gap, Cumberland Mountain's crest is a virtually unbroken, 160-km-long (100-mi-long) ridge along the converging borders of Kentucky, Virginia, and Tennessee. National Park Service photograph by Scott Teodorski (Cumberland Gap National Historical Park).

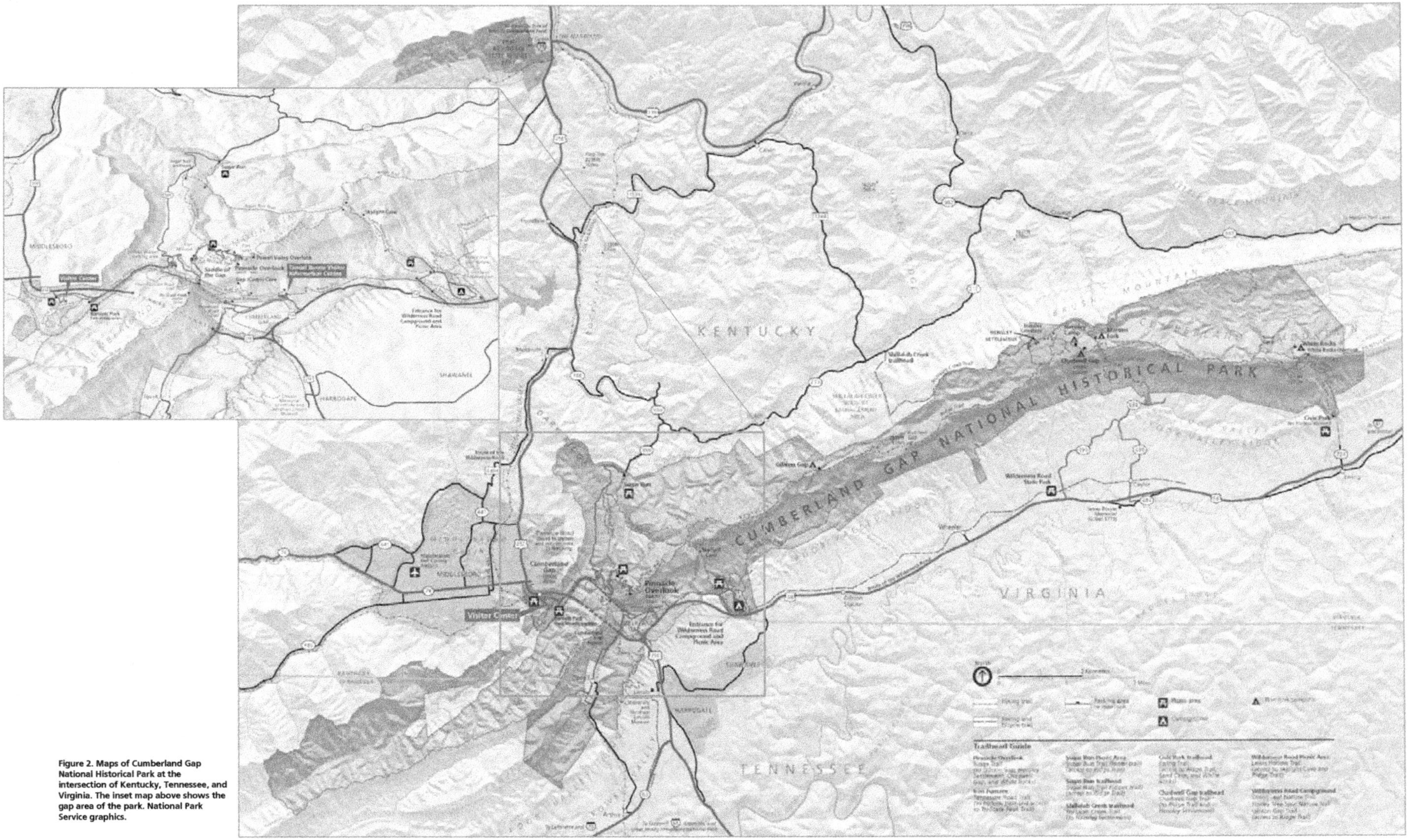

Figure 2. Maps of Cumberland Gap National Historical Park at the intersection of Kentucky, Tennessee, and Virginia. The inset map above shows the gap area of the park. National Park Service graphics.

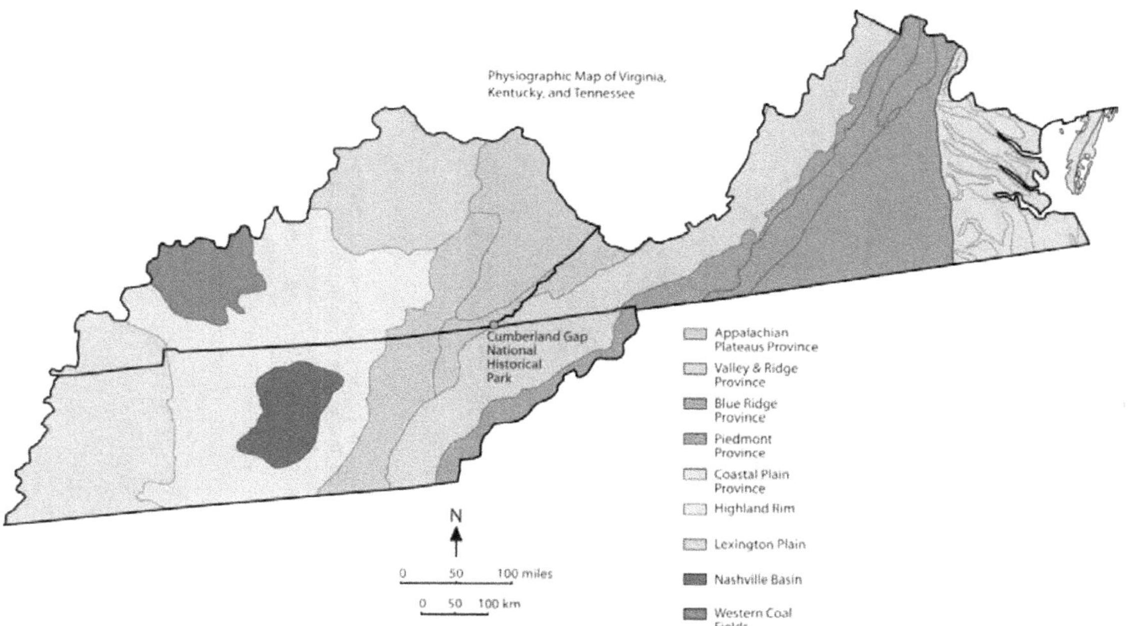

Figure 3. Physiographic provinces. Diagram of physiographic provinces and other features of Virginia, Kentucky, and Tennessee. Green dot indicates the approximate location of Cumberland Gap National Historical Park. Graphic by Trista L. Thornberry-Ehrlich (Colorado State University) with information from the U.S. Geological Survey, College of William and Mary, Kentucky Geological Survey, and Middle Tennessee State University.

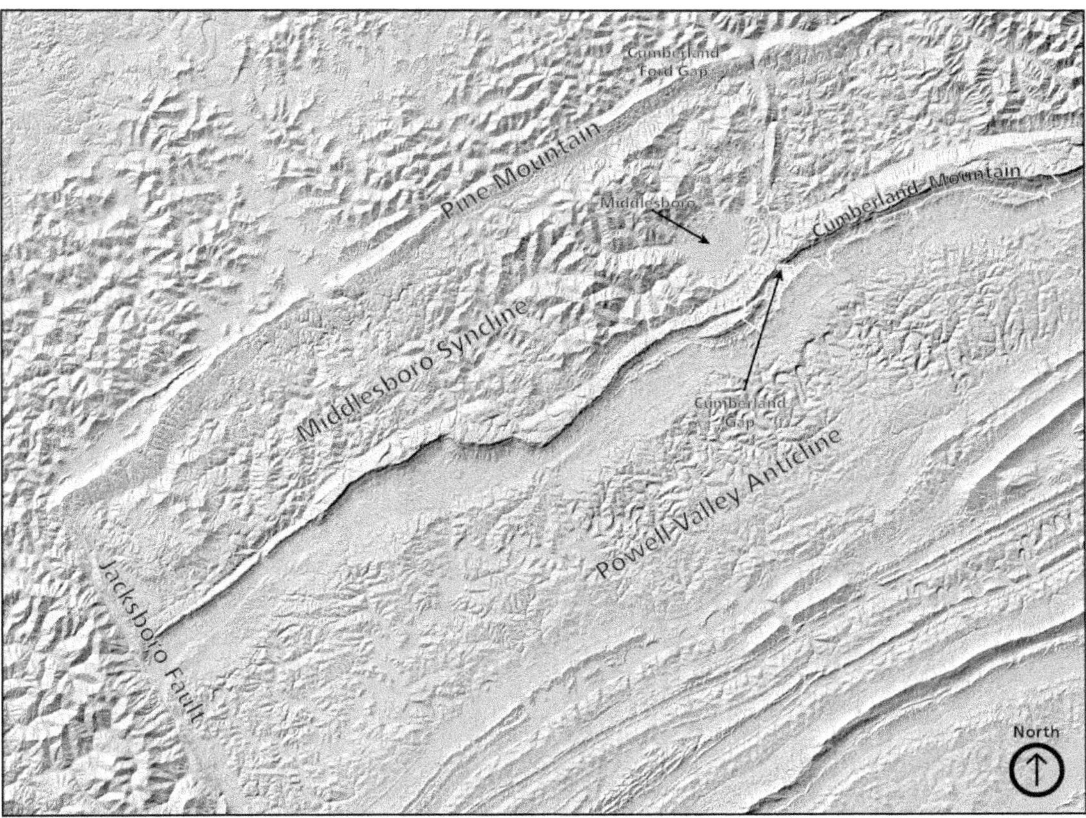

Figure 4. Shaded relief map. This map of the Cumberland Mountain area shows some of the major structural features. Approximate location of the historic Wilderness Road is indicated by dashed orange line. Cumberland Gap National Historical Park is outlined in yellow. Cumberland Ford Gap is also called the Pineville Gap. Graphic by Philip Reiker (NPS Geologic Resources Division) after figure 5 from Dean (1989).

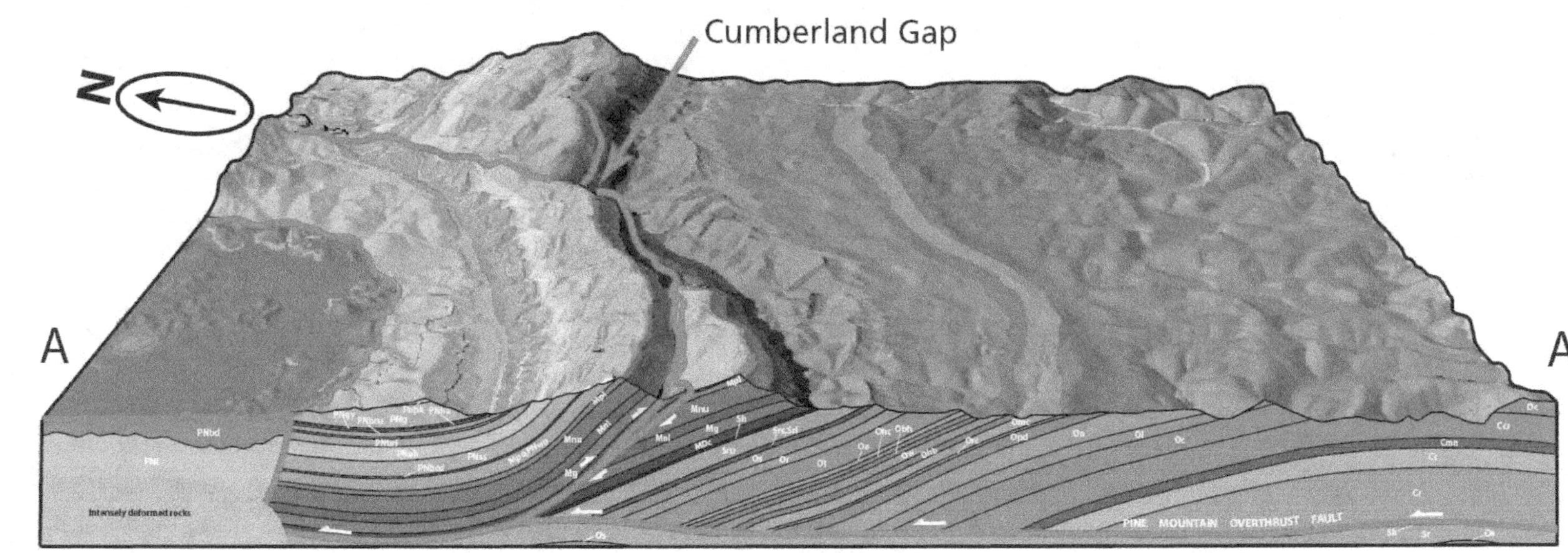

Figure 5. Block diagram of Cumberland Gap area. This diagram depicts the landforms of the park area as well as a cross-section (cross section A-A′ from Englund et al. 1964) that reveals the major geologic structures through the Pine Mountain thrust sheet. Different colors represent different geologic formations. Thick red lines are faults. An ancient fault, the Rocky Face Fault is responsible for the Cumberland Gap. The geologic structures of the area are associated with Appalachian Mountain building processes that occurred hundreds of millions of years ago. Graphic compiled by Philip Reiker (NPS Geologic Resources Division) using digital geologic data (GIS) produced for Cumberland Gap NHP. Cross section redrafted by Trista Thornberry-Ehrlich (Colorado State University).

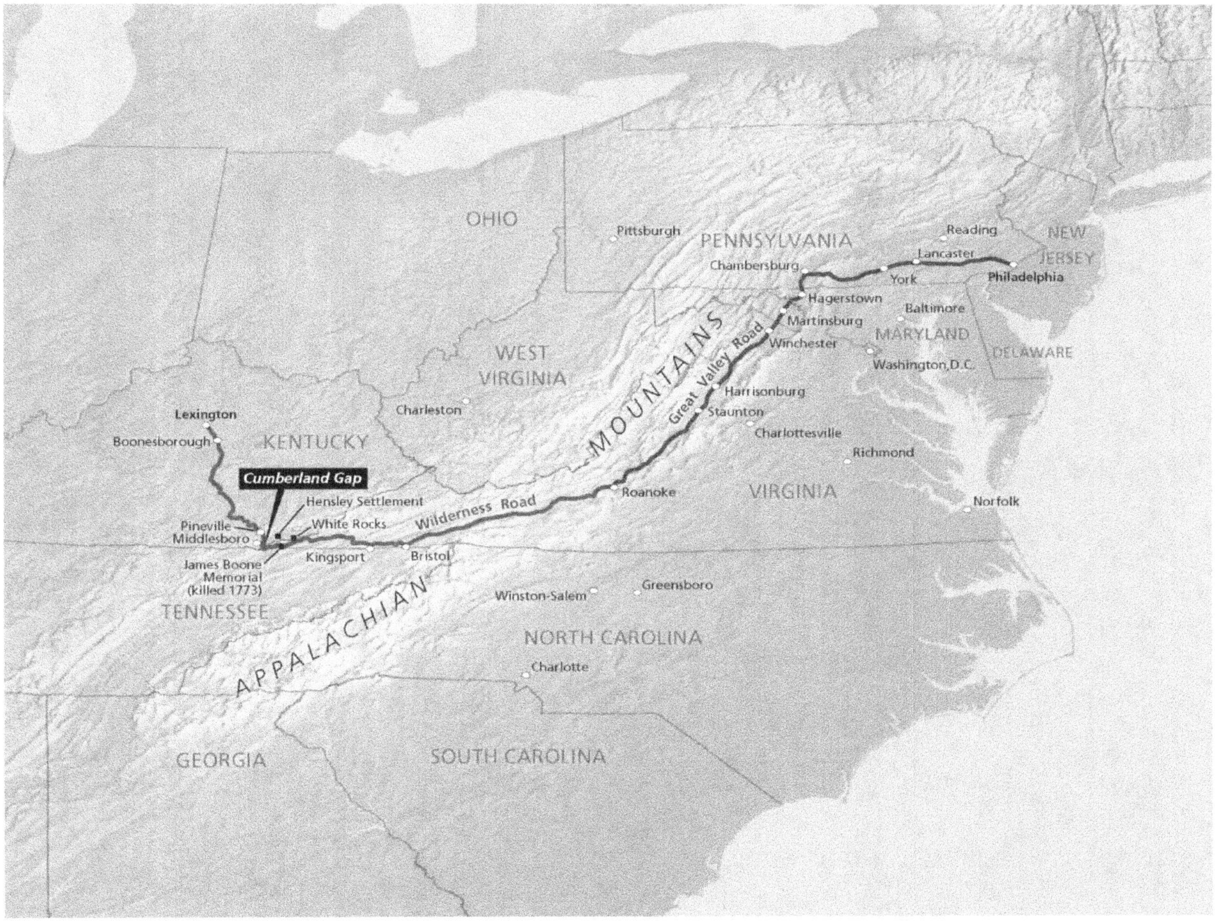

Figure 6. Wilderness Road. Map showing the route of the Wilderness Road during western expansion. National Park Service graphic.

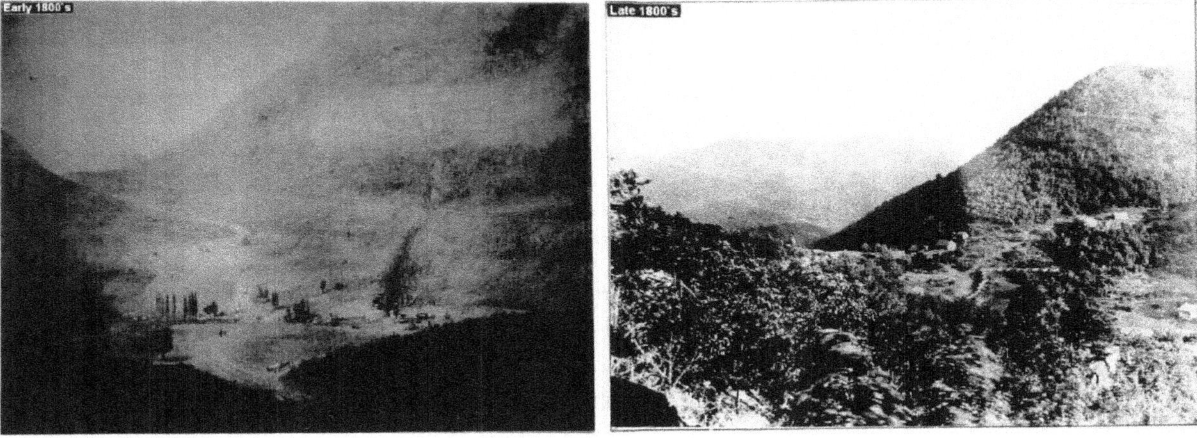

Figure 7. Historic photographs. The photograph on the left (from an obscura print) is believed to be from before 1860 with a view northwest toward the saddle of Cumberland Gap The photograph on the right (taken by Inman Photographers of Middlesboro, Kentucky) is believed to be from the late 1800s with a view south toward the saddle of Cumberland Gap. Note the presence of buildings in the saddle area and the low vegetation resulting from the deforestation during the American Civil War. Photographs courtesy of the National Park Service, presented in Unrau (2002).

Geologic Issues

The Geologic Resources Division held a Geologic Resources Inventory scoping session for Cumberland Gap National Historical Park on June 6 and 7, 2007, to discuss geologic resources, address the status of geologic mapping, and assess resource management issues and needs. This section synthesizes the scoping results, in particular those issues that may require attention from resource managers. Contact the Geologic Resources Division for technical assistance.

At the 2007 Geologic Resources Inventory scoping session, six primary issues were discussed and briefly summarized by Thornberry-Ehrlich (2008):

- Fluvial issues and pH changes in surface waters
- Cave and karst issues
- Mass wasting
- Disturbed lands and adjacent land use
- Fern Lake watershed resource management issues
- Seismicity

Fluvial Issues and pH Changes in Surface Waters

Cumberland Gap National Historical Park contains the headwaters of several large streams that flow downslope from the ridgeline both eastward and westward. These relatively high elevation streams are an important natural resource for the park and contain rare upland bogs and riparian habitat. Fluvial issues include riverbank and head-cutting erosion (Thornberry-Ehrlich 2008). Steep stream courses cause instability during high-energy flows. During high flow events (e.g. following a thunderstorm) the energy of the water may dislodge large boulders and slabs of rock. Streams such as Shillalah Creek contain blocks of cliff-forming sandstone (geologic map unit PNss) as large as passenger buses that have tumbled down the slopes after being undercut by erosion and dislodged by processes such as frost heave and root wedging (fig. 8) (also see the Mass Wasting section) (Thornberry-Ehrlich 2008). Boone Trail, Sugar Run Trail, Lewis Hollow Trail, and Shillalah Creek Trail pass closely to park streams and in certain reaches are threatened by channel erosion and undercutting. Access roads within the park are used by NPS vehicles and motorized equipment (they are not open to the public). These primitive roads are especially prone to erosion which may result in increased sediments washed to park streams.

Lord et al. (2009) provide an overview of river and stream dynamics, describe potential triggers of channel instability, and describe methods to monitor streams and rivers. Stream channel morphology is influenced by complex interrelationships between regional geology, climate, topographic gradient, drainage basin history, river history, and sediment load. Channel instability manifests itself as significant changes in channel bed elevation, cross-sectional morphology, and channel pattern changes. A subset of characteristics of a fluvial system that can be monitored to provide information about the condition and trends of a system, including: 1) watershed landscape (vegetation, land use, surficial geology, slopes, and hydrology), 2) hydrology (frequency, magnitude, and duration of stream flow rates), 3) sediment transport (rates, modes, sources, and types of sediment), 4) channel cross-section, 5) channel planform, and 6) channel longitudinal profile (Lord et al. 2009).

Some streams in the park have low pH levels, resulting in streams devoid of fish and other aquatic life. For example, Martin's Fork and Shillalah Creek have pHs that range from approximately 4.0 to 6.0, compared to an average rainfall pH of approximately 5.6 (J. Beeler, resource management specialist, Cumberland Gap NHP, written communication, October 13, 2011). Values approaching 4.0 are too low (acidic) to sustain healthy aquatic communities (Thornberry-Ehrlich 2008).

The underlying causes of the low pH are not well understood. Acid rain may be a contributing factor, but this alone cannot explain the low pH. Acid mine drainage occurs via the oxidation of metal sulfides (often pyrite, which is iron-sulfide) when the mining-exposed rock and overburden comes into contact with air and water. Acid mine drainage can dramatically lower the pH of a stream, however, there are no mined areas in the headwater regions at the park (Thornberry-Ehrlich 2008). Upland wetlands and pine tree soils may also contribute to lower pH of surface water through decay of organic matter in the water.

The local geologic setting may contribute to the low pH of certain streams. If sulfur-rich shales and coal beds are naturally exposed to water, chemical reactions between iron sulfide and water may discharge sulfuric acid into the stream water. However, if the cause for the acidity were due to the local geology, the streams should have always had low pH. These streams supported documented fish populations in the past; the park has at least a 15-year record of water quality for these and four other streams in the park (the data was mostly collected in conjunction with the work on the tunnel), (Thornberry-Ehrlich 2008; J. Beeler, resource management specialist, Cumberland Gap NHP, written communication, January 2011). More research is needed to understand the cause(s) of low pH levels in the park and how the underlying geology may be a contributor.

For technical assistance regarding water quality issues contact the NPS Water Resources Division (http://nature.nps.gov/water/)

Caves and Karst Issues

A cave is an underground open space (natural or artificial) usually with a connection to the surface that is large enough for a human to enter and long enough to extend into darkness. Karst is a type of topography formed in limestone or dolomite and other soluble rocks primarily through dissolution. Dissolution occurs when acidic groundwater reacts with carbonate rock surfaces, along subterranean cracks and fractures (Palmer 1981; Toomey 2009). Most meteoric water is slightly acidic (relatively low pH) due to the reaction between atmospheric carbon dioxide (CO_2) and water (H_2O). The product of this reaction is carbonic acid (H_2CO_3). Groundwater may become even more acidic as it flows through decaying plant debris and soils. The acid reacts with calcium carbonate ($CaCO_3$) in the rocks to produce soluble calcium (Ca^{2+}) and bicarbonate (HCO^{3-}). The result is that the limestone rocks are dissolved and are "in solution". Over hundreds of thousands of years, dissolution has occurred between the intergranular pores and along fractures in the limestones of the park, creating larger and larger voids. Internal (subterranean) drainage, losing streams (part of the discharge sinks below ground), caves, springs, and sinkholes characterize karst landscapes (Toomey 2009).

At Cumberland Gap, karst dissolution occurs in the tilted, limestone-bearing Mississippian bedrock units as well as other rock units that contain carbonate minerals or carbonate cemented sandstone (see Map Unit Properties Table). Karst features in the park area include caves (Skylight and Gap caves appear on the park map), conduits, sinking springs, gaps, pits, sinkholes (Lewis Hollow area), and springs (such as Cumberland Gap spring). The Powell River Valley, part of the park's viewshed, contains many karst features, developed on Ordovician limestones, south and east of Cumberland Gap (Henry and Crockett 2004; Crockett 2005). Figures 9–11 illustrate some of the karst features that are typical for the area and their modes of formation. However, not all of these features are karst related; some cave features are manmade (ordinance craters and small adits) or natural structural configurations such as overhangs and weathered fractures. Issues associated with the cave and karst features in the park include understanding the groundwater flow through the system, managing the cave resources, and mitigating karst hazards.

Karst Hydrogeology

Dissolution of bedrock within the park creates highly permeable karst conduits and networks. These subterranean drainages (groundwater flow) do not always correspond with the surficial drainage basin divides and thus the watersheds cannot be delineated by topography alone. Groundwater from the subterranean drainages can emerge as karst springs, such as the Cumberland Gap Spring located in Gap Cave (Thornberry-Ehrlich 2008). Water rights are retained through a deed restriction with Lincoln Memorial University in Harrogate, Tennessee (J. Beeler, resource management specialist, Cumberland Gap NHP, written communication, October 13, 2011). Dye tracing studies can delineate the recharge area for a particular spring. The park has interest in more dye trace studies for the local area's karst conduit networks (Thornberry-Ehrlich 2008). As of December 2010, Joe Meiman is the hydrologist for the Cumberland Piedmont Network and a contact point for hydrogeologic assistance (see Appendix for contact information).

Karst aquifers are highly susceptible to contamination because water has a fast transport time from the surface to the aquifer with minimal filtration. Known contamination issues in karst aquifers in Kentucky include suspended sediment and bacteria (Kentucky Geological Survey 2010). Fortunately, Cumberland Gap National Historical Park straddles the top of a watershed so the park has the ability to manage the common sources of these contaminants.

Contaminants such as mercury are readily transported through karst aquifer systems. Atmospheric mercury comes from coal-fired power plants and is deposited in rivers and sediments, and concentrates in organisms through rain, wind, and bioaccumulation. Approximately 94% of Kentucky's electricity comes from coal-fired power plants (Kentucky Department for Energy Development and Independence 2010). Emissions from these plants naturally travel east on prevailing winds towards Cumberland Gap National Historical Park. Regional studies are revealing that mercury is elevated in cave-dwelling bat hair and guano (Clark et al. 2007). Elevated mercury could be an issue at Cumberland Gap National Historical Park.

The Kentucky Geological Survey and other agencies such as the Kentucky Natural Resources and Environmental Protection Cabinet, develop groundwater basin quadrangle maps (see http://www.uky.edu/KGS/). If such products were developed for the Cumberland Gap area, they could be used to quickly identify individual groundwater basins and springs to which a particular surface may drain. The relative size of individual catchment basins can be evaluated as well as potential water supplies and contaminant transport. These types of maps are generated primarily by groundwater tracer studies; however, the precise flow paths are relatively unknown and inferred or interpreted using water-level data, geologic structure, or surficial morphology (Ray and Currens 1998).

Caves

Most of the caves in the park form via karst dissolution of carbonate rock units. Sand Cave (described below) is an exception. The high relief and tilted bedrock units in the area promote the development of cave systems. The tilted beds provide a high hydraulic gradient that moves groundwater through the system quickly. This water is continually refreshed and dissolves the carbonate away.

The southern edge of the Pine Mountain thrust sheet rises some 600 m (1,970 ft) above Powell Valley, exposing 150 m (490 ft) of steeply dipping Newman Limestone (geologic map units Mn, Mnl, Mnu). This exposure contains the park's best known cave: Gap Cave, formerly known as Cudjo's Cave (fig. 12; see below) (Henry and Crockett 2004).

There are at least 30 named caves located in Cumberland Gap National Historical Park including, in addition to Gap Cave, Skylight Cave (with a natural skylight a short distance from the entrance), Sand Cave, and Big Salt Cave. Gap and Big Salt caves are connected in a cave network that is surveyed at more than 26 km (16 mi) long (J. Beeler, resource management specialist, Cumberland Gap NHP, written communication 2008). The significant cave resources at the park are mostly understudied; a cave management plan, such as that developed for Gap Cave would help improve understanding of cave resources at the park (Thornberry-Ehrlich 2008). Although the potential for new discoveries exists, the park staff is aware of most, if not all, cave locations (Henry and Crockett 2004; Crockett 2005). Reinforcing the potential for future cave discoveries, the pilot bore for the Cumberland Gap tunnel encountered two cave openings, the Large Tunnel Cave and the Small Tunnel Cave (Dean 1989).

In 1997, Gap Cave (in the Newman Limestone, Mn, Mnl, Mnu) became part of the park and is gated and used for interpretive tours throughout the year. Around the time of its inclusion, the National Park Service and an advisory group of resource experts developed a cave management plan (Thornberry-Ehrlich 2008). The cave contains beautiful cave formations (speleothems) including flow stones, stalactites, and stalagmites (fig. 12).

Sand Cave (fig. 13) is a large rock shelter not related to karst dissolution. Instead, this feature is in quartz arenite sandstone that forms a steep cliff (geologic map unit PNwp) in the White Rocks area. The cave sits on the northern flank of Cumberland Mountain. Over time, weathering and erosion by seeping water and frost wedging removed the less resistant rock underlying the hard sandstone. The preferential weathering in conjunction with the regional dip of the sedimentary strata created the immense rock overhang that is the largest rock shelter in Kentucky (Thornberry-Ehrlich 2008). The Cave Research Foundation initiated GIS-based cave mapping, and is remapping Gap Cave as part of a multidisciplinary study at Gap Cave that began in 2003 (Crockett 2005).

Locations of caves are considered sensitive information due to the risk of vandalism and looting. Past vandalism is evident in most of the larger caves. Gates block the larger openings to prevent visitor access and potential negative impacts on cave resources. The Federal Cave Resources Protection Act of 1988 and its subsequent regulations restrict the release of cave locations except where there is particular need. This law also protects cave location information from Freedom of Information Act requests. Working with law enforcement and employing photomonitoring could possibly help alleviate damage from vandals (Andrea Croskrey, geologist-GIS specialist, NPS Geologic Resources Division, written communication, December 2010).

Caves provide habitat for many species at Cumberland Gap including amphibians, beetles and the threatened and endangered Indiana bat. In order to protect cave resources and maintain habitats for cave dwelling fauna, there is no artificial lighting in the caves. Caves may also contain significant archaeological artifacts and cultural resources. In Soldiers Cave, American Civil War soldiers carved graffiti on the cave walls. These resources associated with caves require protection from degradation and vandalism. Detailed mapping of all park caves could reveal isolated biological communities with specialized species as well as additional archaeological remains. At present, the biological communities of the park's caves are threatened by a fungus infection known as white nose syndrome (National Park Service 2010). This has caused the deaths of more than one million bats throughout the eastern United States. In 2010, Skylight Cave was closed and Gap Cave was open only for guided tours, with restrictions to prevent potentially contaminated clothing from contaminating the cave (National Park Service 2010).

Karst Hazards

Karst-related hazards include sinkhole development and radon gas concentration. The Lewis Hollow area has several sinkholes and sinking streams. At this location, southeast-directed drainage flows below the ground through karst generated conduits of the Newman Limestone (geologic map units Mn, Mnl, Mnu) (Thornberry-Ehrlich 2008). Sinkhole subsidence and development are always possibilities in the area. The Powell River Valley along the eastern flank of Cumberland Mountain is primarily a karst plain of diverse carbonate structures with high potential for sinkhole development as well as cave exploration (Crockett 2005).

Radon is a colorless, odorless, radioactive gas that naturally accumulates in caves throughout the southeast. The confinement inside caves causes radiation levels to be appreciably higher than outside (Yarborough 1981). The decay of radioactive isotopes (uranium-238 and thorium-232) forms radon. Both isotopes naturally occur in the bedrock of the park, particularly the Chattanooga Shale (geologic map unit MDc) (Smith et al. 1997; Environmental Protection Agency 1993). Cave airflow mobilizes radon gas. Airflow is seasonally variable as a function of interior cave and exterior ambient temperatures and pressures as well as the cave's configuration (Yarborough 1980). Radon-222 has a half-life of 3.8 days meaning it could possibly be a concern even after leaving the cave. Radioactivity levels are higher in Gap Cave during the summer when the cool cave air sinks and flows out of the lower Gap Cave openings (J. Beeler, resource management specialist, Cumberland Gap NHP, written communication, October 12, 2011). In winter, there is a modest reversal of air flow and subsequent radiation levels drop (Yarborough 1980). Cumberland Gap National Historical Park has long been concerned about the potential for radon accumulation within the caves. The park has conducted research and monitors radiation levels and employee exposure (Yarborough 1980, 1981). The exposure standard used by the NPS is 3 working level months (WLM) per year. Working Level Month is defined as a unit of radon exposure equivalent to one working level of radon decay products for one working month (170 hours) (Smith et al. 1997). Scoping participants in 2007 were not concerned about the exposure levels at Cumberland Gap National Historical Park; however radon exposure remains an issue for resource managers and regional cavers to be aware of.

Toomey (2009) describes caves and karst landscapes as well as methods to inventory and monitor cave-related vital signs. Vital signs are measurable parameters of the overall condition of the cave system and include: 1) cave meteorology (microclimate and air composition of the cave), 2) airborne sedimentation (dust and lint), 3) direct visitor impacts (breakage of cave formations, trail use in caves, graffiti, cave lighting, etc.), 4) permanent or seasonal ice, 5) cave drip and pool water (drip locations, drip rate, drip volume, drip water chemistry, microbiology, and temperature), 6) microbiology, 7) stability-breakdown, rockfall and partings, 8) mineral growth (speleothems such as stalagmites and stalactites), 9) surface expressions and processes (karst processes link the surface to caves through springs, sinkholes, cracks, etc.), 10) regional groundwater levels and quantity, and 11) fluvial processes (underground streams and rivers) (Toomey 2009). The Cave Research Foundation enters caves throughout the area to complete surveys and inventories (J. Beeler, resource management specialist, Cumberland Gap NHP, written communication, January 2011).

Mass Wasting

Mass wasting refers to the dislodging and downslope movement of soil and rock material. Mass wasting processes in the park are exacerbated by natural geologic features and processes as well as infrastructure development and other anthropogenic activities.

Steep slopes characterize the landscape of Cumberland Gap National Historical Park and are especially prone to mass wasting events including landslides, block falls, slumps, and debris flows. Slides may be caused by one or more factors, of which geological, morphological, physical, and anthropogenic factors are most common (Wieczorek and Snyder 2009). Gravity, frost heaving, root wedging, erosion, and karst dissolution are among the primary causes of natural slope instability. Features within the bedrock such as regional dip, undercut sandstones, pervasive fractures, weathered exposures, and thick and weak shale units create unstable settings on steep to moderate slopes. Groundwater seeps create localized areas of weakness (Thornberry-Ehrlich 2008). The NPS Geologic Resources Division completed an evaluation of geohazards at Cumberland Gap National Historical Park (Greco 2006). This report addressed Gap Cave and the Wilderness Road slump, which are described below.

Some geologic units, such as the Chattanooga Shale(geologic map unit Oc), contain soluble intergranular carbonate cements. When the cements between grains dissolve away, the entire unit is rendered friable and prone to increased mass wasting and erosion (Thornberry-Ehrlich 2008). The Chattanooga Shale exposed in the lowermost elevations of the park area, is structurally weak and is especially prone to faulting and landsliding where exposed on slopes (Thornberry-Ehrlich 2008).

Landslide units (geologic map unit Qls) are mapped outside of the park boundary. However, other surficial geologic units associated with mass wasting are mapped (in places where the deposit is more than 3 m [10 ft] thick) within the park as colluvium or colluvial soil (geologic map unit Qc) (Englund 1964; Rice and Maughan 1978). To some degree, colluvium mantles the base of all the slopes in the park. These types of deposits indicate areas where large-scale mass wasting has occurred and may continue to occur in the future. Block slides are common in the park area, but most landslide activity occurs within colluvial deposits (M. Crawford, geologist, Kentucky Geological Survey, written communication, May 2011).

Mass wasting near cave openings is another geologic hazard associated with park caves, particularly Gap Cave. Rockfall (fractured limestone) near the portal of Gap Cave threaten the safety of visitors on interpretive tours. A large rockfall event in 1999 prompted the construction of an engineered support structure at the cave's entrance. Currently, two pillars support a rock slab that is already detached, fractured, poorly supported and may fail (fig. 14). Loose boulders and talus litter the slopes above the entrance and exit to the cave. These frequently fall onto the trail below these cave openings especially when there is heavy rainfall. They may also be loosened by frost and root wedging, freeze and thaw cycles, crystal growth, temperature changes (cycles of expansion and contraction), and gravity (Cloues 1999). NPS mining engineer Phil Cloues recommended long-term monitoring, properly removing unstable high-hazard rocks from the slopes, and constructing a suitable tunnel lining near the cave's entrance to provide needed support. Greco (2006) recommended 1) placement of an extensometer at the cave entrance to monitor the rock wedge perched above the entrance, 2) signage and interpretive information about mass wasting, 3) avoid queuing people near the entrance for any period of time, and 4) document rockfall incidents to determine trigger patterns. Pillars were installed after the rockfall to provide some support to the bedrock (fig. 15).

Beyond the natural factors contributing to mass wasting, human activities such as landscaping, road construction, and facilities development may cause mass wasting. Cutting into the toe of a slope or loading the top of a slope may render it unstable and susceptible to sliding. Diverting water into certain areas may exacerbate local erosion or saturate slopes. Within the last decade, mass wasting in the park occurred at the entrance to the Wilderness Road campground, along the trail to Gap Cave, near the Cumberland Gap tunnel, Thomas Walker parking lot. A slide-prone area within the park, along the south side of Highway 25E, beyond the tunnel toward Harrogate, Tennessee required shotcrete and bolts to stabilize the slope. There are slope monitors at the top of the area to determine if the slope is moving further (J. Beeler, resource management specialist, Cumberland Gap NHP, written communication, January 2011).

Prior to restoring the Wilderness Road, old Highway 25E experienced regular slumping through Cumberland Gap; seeps and springs were visible along the road corridor (Greco 2006). The restoration of Wilderness Road (see "Disturbed Lands" below) did not completely remove old drainage structures from the former highway and these structures now concentrate runoff and can trigger mass wasting. Active slumping, caused by the steep, reconstructed slope, abundant fill material, and lack of forest for root stability, disrupts the Wilderness Road trail requiring repeated maintenance of a section of slope adjacent to and below the trail (figs. 16 and 17) (Greco 2006; Thornberry-Ehrlich 2008). The park may consider reconstructing and reinforcing rock buttresses beneath the Wilderness Road trailbed to increase stability there. As of 2006, rock buttresses were in place to support the trailbed, but were located near the upper portion of the slide. Rock buttresses are most effective when constructed at the toe of a slide, nearer to the bottom of the slope (Greco 2006). As the slope naturally revegetates, it will become more stable, but construction of rock buttresses at the toe of the slide (extending several feet beyond the lateral extents of the slide) would greatly increase slope stability (Greco 2006).

Wieczorek and Snyder (2009) described the various types of slope movements and mass wasting triggers. They suggested five methods along with vital signs for monitoring slope movements: types of landslides, landslide triggers and causes, geologic materials in landslides, measurement of landslide movement and assessing landslide hazards and risks. Their publication provides guidance using vital signs and monitoring methodology. As mentioned above under "Karst Hydrogeology", the Kentucky Geological Survey is producing GIS-based land-use planning maps derived from geologic maps for Cumberland Gap National Historical Park (Crawford et al. 2008). These maps relate rock types to various issues including mass wasting. Such a product is a valuable tool for resource managers to help predict and understand potential mass wasting hazard areas.

Cumberland Gap Tunnel

The Cumberland Gap tunnel opened in 1996, completing a rerouting project for Highway 58 and Highway 25E. The tunnel complex contains twin, two-lane, 1,250-m-long (4,100-ft-long), 12-m-wide (40-ft-wide) tunnels through Cumberland Mountain (Abramson 1993). The park owns the tunnel, which crosses a large karst area, but the states of Tennessee and Kentucky, and the Federal Highway Administration are responsible for maintaining the roadway (Thornberry-Ehrlich 2008). The pilot bore gave geologists unique opportunities to study the geology of Cumberland Mountain from complete exposures inside the mountain (Dean 1989). The initial exploration revealed the presence of coal, methane gas, solution features, caverns, and groundwater under pressure (Abramson 1993). The excavation of the highway destroyed the pilot bore (became the southbound lane) and the rocks exposed by the tunnel construction are now covered by artificial materials (Dean 1989; M. Crawford, geologist, Kentucky Geological Survey, written communication, May 2011).

The site is remote, mountainous, and environmentally sensitive, therefore the geotechnical exploration and design of the tunnel was a complicated process that had to account for local geologic processes (Abramson 1993). For example, the tunnel sits on a suspended floor base to allow it to accommodate any significant seismic shaking. Managing the groundwater flowing through the heavily fractured rocks inside Cumberland Mountain was another engineering challenge. An impermeable layer lines the upper surface of the tunnel, funneling away water percolating from above. The floor of the tunnel incorporates drainage tubes in order to channel subsurface water flow away from the tunnel and roadway (Thornberry-Ehrlich 2008).

During high precipitation events, water percolating down through the fractured bedrock can overwhelm the engineered drainage system of the tunnel. This is causing localized erosion and undercutting around the tunnel entrances, and may threaten the integrity of the tunnel's road surface (Thornberry-Ehrlich 2008). The geologic units (including the Pennington Group, geologic map unit Mp) surrounding the tunnel contain shrink-and-swell clays. These clays expand when saturated with water and contract upon drying. The volume changes associated with these clays in the coal and shale units around the tunnel may eventually undermine its structural integrity (Thornberry-Ehrlich 2008). Ground penetrating radar and dye tracing indicate the presence of a naturally occurring cavern in the soluble carbonate units beneath the roadway. These techniques also indicate that voids are developing beneath the roadway (Thornberry-Ehrlich 2008). If the extent of these voids continues to increase, the stability and integrity of the roadway may be threatened and park resources may be impacted.

A 9.7-ha (24-ac) outflow area for the drainage system from the tunnel is on privately owned land in the town of Cumberland Gap, Tennessee. This private land was previously the site of a construction debris dump. The park has some concerns that the debris in this former dump area may clog the drainage system outlet for the tunnel (Thornberry-Ehrlich 2008). Currently, because the site is on private property, the park does not monitor or maintain the system (J. Beeler, resource management specialist, Cumberland Gap NHP, written communication, January 2011).

Disturbed Lands

Coal and iron-ore mining have been important regional industries for more than 100 years and continue today. Smaller-scale quarrying of limestone and sandstone also occurs. Disturbed lands within the park—old (ca. approximately 1900) coal mines and iron mines, potassium nitrate mines, abandoned haul access roads, and a few sand and gravel quarries—were not large-scale mines or quarries, but do attest to the importance of mining to the history of the Cumberland Gap area (Englund 1964; Thornberry-Ehrlich 2008). Locally, much of the coal mined is from the Pennsylvanian Breathitt Group (see Map Unit Properties Table and Geologic Map Overview). The Cumberland Gap coal bed (geologic map unit PNbcdcg) and Tunnel coal bed (within unit PNah) appear in outcrop on the northwest slope of Cumberland Mountain. Small mine workings are caved in and obscured. The steep dip of the beds (between 24 and 60°) and extensive fracturing likely discouraged further mining operations (Englund 1964). The Mason and Hance coal beds of the Breathitt Group (geologic map units PNgma and PNha, respectively) were extensively prospected and mined in the park area. Larger coal mines are visible from overlooks within the park such as the Pinnacle (fig. 18). Sedimentary hematite beds (also called oolitic hematite deposits) within the Rockwood Formation (geologic map unit Sr) were a source of iron ore in early mining operations. Pre-1900 iron furnaces in the Cumberland Gap area rivaled production from Pittsburgh, Pennsylvania, but the local source of iron ore was insufficient to maintain long-term production (Englund 1964; Thornberry-Ehrlich 2008). Most of these small-scale mines are now caved in (Englund 1964). Crushed limestone, extracted from outcrop belts of the Woodway, Trenton, and Newman limestones (geologic map units Ow, Ot, and Mn, respectively), and sand mined from a few small open pits within weathered outcrops of sandstone (map units may include PNbr, PNah, PNss, and PNwp) in the Cumberland Gap area (unclear if within the park) were likely local sources of construction material (Englund 1964).

Transportation and access have always been associated with Cumberland Gap. Today, access roads, including old mining roads, unofficial ATV trails, and some maintained as fire roads cross through the rugged, mountainous area as well as along the northwestern side of the Little Yellow Creek drainage. Some access roads (closed to the public) are used by NPS service vehicles. These primitive roads are prone to erosion resulting in increased sediment loads in park streams. The impact of these local access roads is relatively limited and not a source of immediate concern to park resource managers (Thornberry-Ehrlich 2008).

Following completion of the Cumberland Gap tunnel, the park began restoration of the Wilderness Road across the original Cumberland Gap. The goal of this project was to restore historical contours (ca. 1788) of the original route through the gap (fig. 19). Historic accounts and early photographs (fig. 7) aided the restoration. Photographs from the 1800s were applicable because the land contours had not been significantly altered from the late 1700s. The project involved removal of all traces of the previous highway including 9 m (28 ft) of fill material along 6.3 km (3.9 mi) and unearthing what is believed to be the historical trace of the Wilderness Road (Thornberry-Ehrlich 2008). The reconstructed slope now experiences regular slumping along reaches that have not yet established stabilizing forest vegetation (Greco 2006).

White Rocks

The cliffs at White Rocks attract rock climbers (fig. 20). Climbing groups occasionally submit requests to the park to permit climbing there. The long pitches and scenic value of the White Rocks area is very attractive to this sort of visitor use; however, the rock is highly fractured and friable rendering it a relatively poor climbing surface (Greco 2006; Thornberry-Ehrlich 2008). Rock-climbing activity has occurred sporadically without the direct knowledge or consent of park management; according to the park compendium, rock climbing, free climbing or bouldering is prohibited (Greco 2006; J. Beeler, resource management specialist, Cumberland Gap NHP, written communication, January 2011). If climbing were allowed at White Rocks, there would be the potential for degradation of the rock face from drilling anchors, and for local vegetation to be trampled at the top and bottom of the climbing routes (J. Beeler, resource management specialist, Cumberland Gap NHP, written communication, 2008.

Inventory projects, including one by Appalachian State University in 2005–2006, indicate that there are at least 14 different vascular plants associated with the White Rocks cliffs, one of which is endangered—the silvery nailwort (*Paronychia argyrocoma*) (Walker et al. 2007; J. Beeler, resource management specialist, Cumberland Gap NHP, written communication, 2008 and January 2011). Forty-eight species of lichen thrive on the cliff face of White Rocks; several lichen species were biogeographically rare, relict, disjunct, or represent new habitat occurrences for their taxons (J. Beeler, resource management specialist, Cumberland Gap NHP, written communication, January 2011). One species in particular is unique to the area—a foliose lichen (*Umbilicaria torrefacta*), normally found in northern Canada and Alaska with subdistributions in the northwestern mountains and Rocky Mountains. This is the first report of this species in the southeastern United States (J. Beeler, resource management specialist, Cumberland Gap NHP, written communication, January 2011). Greco (2006) recommends hazard mitigation such as warning signs, physical barriers, educational programs, and localized closure to protect White Rocks. Regular monitoring of soil compaction, erosion potential, and vegetation would also help understand impacts to the resources at White Rocks (Greco 2006).

Contact the Geologic Resources Division for technical assistance regarding disturbed lands restoration.

Fern Lake Watershed Water and Mineral Resource Issues

In 2004, Cumberland Gap National Historical Park was authorized to initiate acquisition of approximately 1,820 ha (4,500 ac) including the dam-impounded Fern Lake Reservoir and the Little Yellow Creek watershed in Kentucky and Tennessee (fig. 18). Water from Fern Lake Reservoir is the public water supply for Middlesboro, Kentucky. The rights to the water, along with the dam and all appurtenances (incidental rights or right-of-ways) associated with the withdrawal and delivery of water from the lake will be given to the city of Middlesboro (Thornberry-Ehrlich 2008). Currently, a private individual owns the dam and is responsible for maintenance. The park participates in regular inspections as an interested party (J. Beeler, resource management specialist, Cumberland Gap NHP, written communication, January 2011).

Coal mining, both past and present, has played a major role in the economic development of the Cumberland Gap-Middlesboro area. The park does not own the mineral rights to the Fern Lake tract. Privately owned mineral resources may be a future target for mineral development of coal, oil and gas (Thornberry-Ehrlich 2008). Although the National Park Service does not own the mineral rights in the area, the NPS does have legal authority to provide input during the permitting process of mining activities within park viewsheds. The Surface Mining Control and Reclamation Act of 1977 controls surface coal mining and reclamation activities on both federal and non-federal lands. Surface coal mining includes activities conducted on the land surface in connection with a surface coal mine or surface operations and impacts associated with an underground mine. Section 522(e) of this Act contains provisions that protect "publicly owned parks" from adverse impacts of surface coal mining on lands within the boundaries of parks, unless there are "valid existing rights." In 1996 the Department of the Interior used the provisions of the Surface Mining Control and Reclamation Act of 1977 to protect the water and viewshed along the park's Tennessee border by prohibiting surface coal mining. This directive was fueled by input from park and other NPS staff, local citizens, and the National Parks Conservation Association regarding the potential impacts to park viewshed, water quality, and endangered species (McCoy 1996). Subsequent to the decision regarding mining on Tennessee lands within the Fern Lake area, the park was engaged in legal proceedings to halt new surface mining in the Kentucky portion. The proposed location would have also been visible from the Pinnacle Overlook (J. Beeler, resource management specialist, Cumberland Gap NHP, written communication, January 2011). The park is interested in developing mineral management plan to address current and future issues.

Oil and/or gas wells are also present in the Fern Lake acquisition area (Thornberry-Ehrlich 2008). Two active wells are within the Fern Lake watershed and one pipeline easement that passes over the ridge near Baptist Gap. Any proposed new wells will be subject to environmental impact compliance studies (J. Beeler, resource management specialist, Cumberland Gap NHP, written communication, January 2011).

At depth, the source for the hydrocarbons in the Cumberland Gap area (and the Appalachian Basin) is the organic deposits within the Chattanooga Shale (geologic map unit MDc). Gas-producing rocks of the Newman Limestone and Pennington Group rocks (see Map Unit Properties Table) are exposed within the park. Wilpolt and Marden (1959) described such rocks in southwestern Virginia and eastern Kentucky. Petroleum and gas reservoirs only occur at depth. Within the park area the Chattanooga Shale is exposed. However, it may serve as a useful analog for models of other buried shale systems and facilitate oil and gas development in surrounding areas where the shale is still buried. Gas exploration is a possibility for Mississippian-aged rocks surrounding the park. The NPS Geologic Resources Division is a source for policy and technical support to parks involved with minerals development both inside and outside the park boundaries.

Seismicity

Compared to areas along active plate margins (e.g. the San Andreas fault in California) large earthquakes are not prevalent in the Cumberland Gap area. This is expected along the relatively passive eastern margin of the North American continent. However, small earthquake events do occur regularly along local faults, some of which were previously unknown (Thornberry-Ehrlich 2008). The Cumberland Gap tunnel sits on a suspended floor base to allow it to accommodate any significant seismic shaking indicating awareness of seismic potential by the developers. According to the U.S. Geological Survey's national seismic hazard map of 2008, Cumberland Gap National Historical Park sits in an area of moderate hazard that trends along the eastern margin of Tennessee south into Georgia (Peterson et al. 2008a, 2008b).

Due to the frequency and probability of significant seismic movement along the eastern margin of Tennessee as far north as Cumberland Gap, geologists refer to the area as the Eastern Tennessee seismic zone. It is one of the most active seismic zones in eastern North America with more than 44 detectable earthquakes since 1982 (Chapman et al. 2002). The Eastern Tennessee seismic zone has earthquake events that are detectable by people on the surface at the park, usually ranging in magnitude from 3 to 4 (Chapman et al. 2002; M. Crawford, geologist, Kentucky Geological Survey, written communication, May 2011). Earthquakes occur in response to tectonic stresses on basement structures deep beneath the earth's surface. Intra-plate seismic zones are much less understood than seismicity at tectonic plate boundaries. The U.S. Geological Survey detected a magnitude 4.9 earthquake within the Eastern Tennessee seismic zone in 2003 (M. Crawford, geologist, Kentucky Geological Survey, written communication,

May 2011). The focal depths of most earthquakes in this zone range from 5 to 22 km (3 to 13 mi), beneath large Paleozoic-aged detachment surfaces (faults) (Chapman et al. 2002). In the park area, the Pine Mountain thrust sheet is the principal detachment surface, but is probably not the source of today's earthquakes. Fault movement within the Eastern Tennessee seismic zone is primarily lateral (strike-slip) movement with right-lateral motion on north-south trending faults and left-lateral motion on east-west trending faults (Chapman et al. 2002). The largest historical magnitude was 4.6 in 1973 (Chapman et al. 2002) and a recent event, on July 20, 1997, was close to a magnitude 4. The U.S. Geological Survey detected a magnitude 4.9 earthquake within the Eastern Tennessee seismic zone in 2003 (M. Crawford, geologist, Kentucky Geological Survey, written communication, May 2011). On August 23, 2011 a magnitude 5.8 earthquake occurred in the nearby Central Virginia Seismic Zone outside of Charlottesville, Virginia. While damage was mostly localized near the epicenter, the quake could be felt throughout the eastern U.S. from Georgia to central Maine, and even in many parts of southeastern Canada. The park is close enough to the New Madrid seismic zone (in western Tennessee) that effects from the large 1811–1812 earthquakes were likely felt in the park, but not necessarily documented as significant (J. Beeler, resource management specialist, Cumberland Gap NHP, written communication, January 2011).

The U.S. Geological Survey maintains an earthquake monitoring website: http://earthquake.usgs.gov/eqcenter/recenteqsus/ as well as a earthquake hazards site: http://earthquake.usgs.gov/hazards/. The KGS has a record of historic earthquake locations for the state of Kentucky at the following website: http://www.uky.edu/KGS/geologichazards/index.htm .

Additional Geologic Map Products

In addition to the digital geologic map product produced by the Geologic Resources Inventory Program (see Geologic Map Data section), a variety of additional products are available through the Kentucky Geological Survey. These products may be useful for resource management efforts within the park.

The Kentucky Geological Survey (KGS) recently produced county-wide, GIS-based land-use planning products derived from many different types of geologic maps (Crawford et al. 2008; M. Crawford, geologist, Kentucky Geological Survey, written communication 2010). These products relate rock types and topography to various hydrologic, environmental, and geohazard issues. For cave and karst areas such as Cumberland Gap National Historical Park, such a product includes relevance to karst geomorphology, cave development, groundwater sensitivity, and plant diversity as a cumulative inventory of the park's geologic issues (Crawford et al. 2008). There are hard-copy maps available for purchase or available for digital download as a PDF (KGS website: http://www.uky.edu/KGS/). The Kentucky Geological Survey has also produced a geologic map of Mammoth Cave National Park, and is working on one for Cumberland Gap National Historical Park, as a comprehensive inventory of geologic issues specific to the park. The geologic maps, based on the county land-use planning map series, are for the "non-geologist" designed to inform the users of geologic/land-use planning issues of the area (M. Crawford, geologist, Kentucky Geological Survey, written communication 2010).

Figure 8. Dislodged boulders. Large boulders in the Shillalah Stream channel are probably of Sewanee Sandstone (geologic map unit PNss). These boulders are dislodged by frost- and root-wedging and tumble downslope. High-energy flow events further transport the boulders. National Park Service photograph by Lisa Norby (NPS Geologic Resources Division).

Rainwater and groundwater percolate through underground fissures and bedding planes, dissolving carbonate minerals, creating wider cavities and conduits.

Conduits continue to widen, creating underground network of cavities, frequently along one or more discrete zones. Larger conduits have larger flows and enlarge faster. Flow moves toward the local base level.

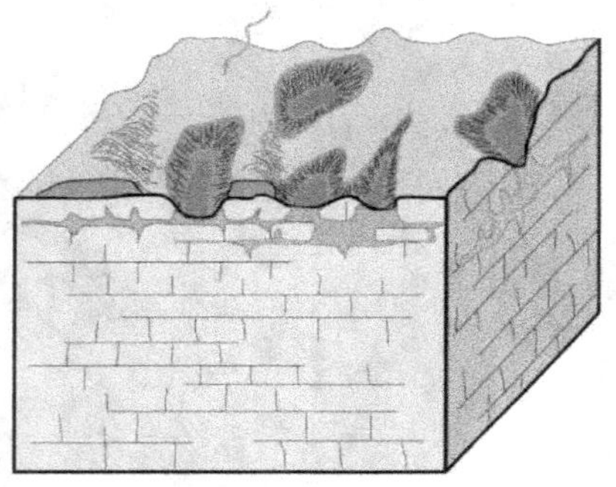

Rocks above cavities and voids subside or (less frequently) collapse forming dissolution holes and sinkholes. Lake and rivers may disappear underground.

Sinkholes overlap and eventually fill with surficial debris. Soils develop and vegetation is established across a rolling landscape. At the soil and bedrock interface, the chemical controls on conduit enlargement concentrate.

Figure 9. Karst landscape development. This schematic cross-sectional view of the development of a karst landscape is analogous to the Lewis Hollow (within park boundaries) and Powell River Valley (within the park's viewshed) areas. Graphic by Trista L. Thornberry-Ehrlich (Colorado State University).

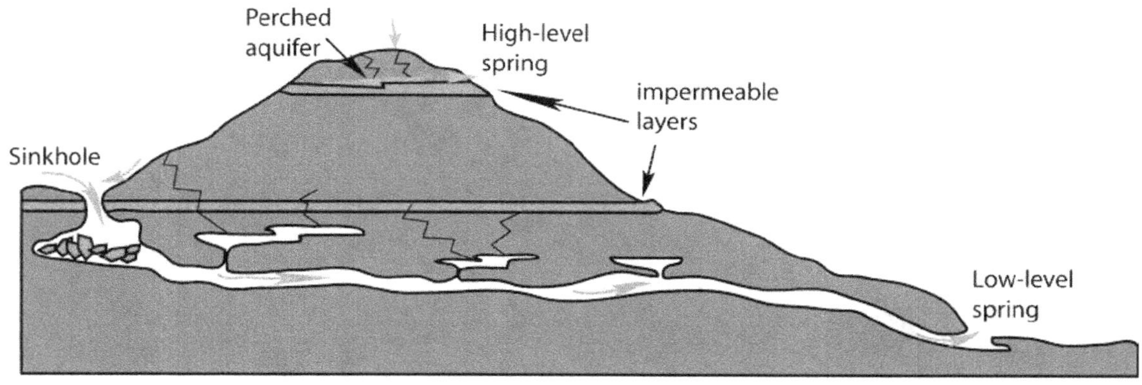

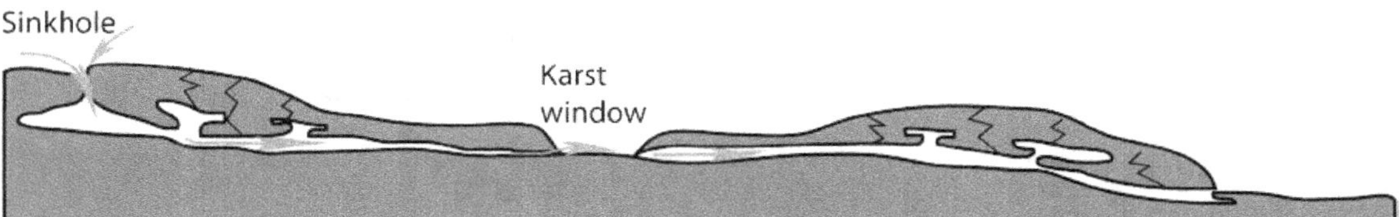

Figure 10. Karst springs. These schematic cross-sectional diagrams illustrate flow paths of springs in a karst landscape. High-level springs discharge from shallow flow paths. Low-level springs incorporate discharge from long, deep conduits. Graphic by Trista L. Thornberry-Ehrlich (Colorado State University) with information from figure 14 of Scanlon and Thrailkill (1987).

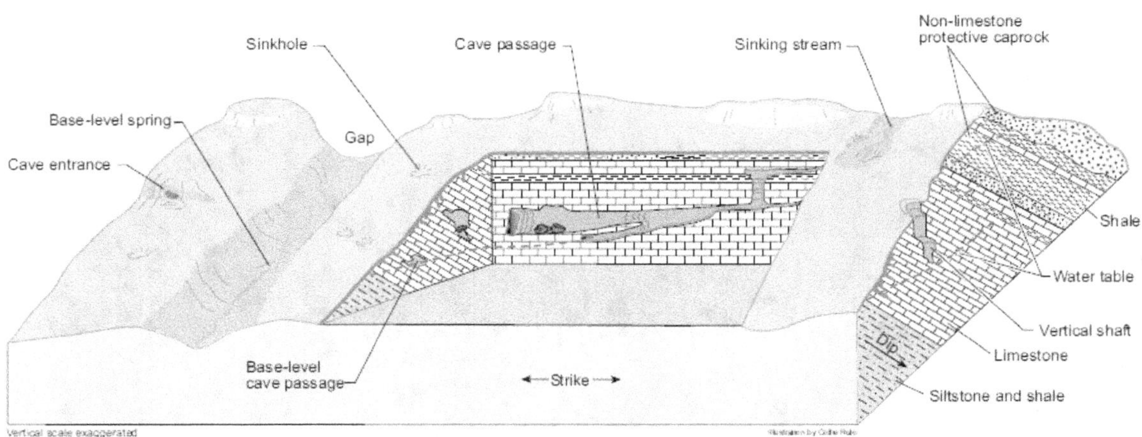

Figure 11. Karst development and features. This generalized block diagram illustrates features of karst development within tilted limestone layers such as at Pine Mountain. Kentucky Geological Survey graphic by Currens (2001).

Figure 12. Gap Cave. Gap Cave formed within the Newman Limestone (geologic map units Mn, Mnl, Mnu) and is a well-decorated karst cave. Colored staining on the walls is commonly due to mineral precipitates deposited by dripping water. Black staining may be manganese oxide. National Park Service photograph by Scott Teodorski (Cumberland Gap National Historical Park).

Figure 13. Sand Cave. Unlike Gap Cave (above), Sand Cave is a non-karst feature that developed at the base of the Warren Point Sandstone (geologic map unit PNwp) . The floor slopes from back to front and has 0.5 ha (1.25 ac) of fine, colorful sand while the open half-domed chamber is 76 m (250 ft) across in front. It is the largest rock shelter in Kentucky, note the hiker for scale. Photograph by Scott Teodorski (Cumberland Gap National Historical Park).

Figure 14. Rockfall at Gap Cave. Following a blockfall event in 1999, debris litters the entrance of Gap Cave. National Park Service photographs by Phil Cloues (NPS Geologic Resources Division).

Figure 15. Gap Cave pillars. Following the blockfall event of 1999 (fig. 14), pillars were installed at the entrance to Gap Cave the pillars for stabilization. Note the large, fractured rock above the pillars, and the trail leading into the cave. National Park Service photograph by Deanna Greco (NPS Geologic Resources Division).

Figure 16. Slump area. Photograph of an area along the restored Wilderness Road that is prone to slumping. Rip rap (arrow) was installed in an effort to stabilize the slope. National Park Service photograph by Lisa Norby (NPS Geologic Resources Division).

Figure 17. Slump boulders. These large boulders are below the slumped area along restored Wilderness Road. National Park Service photograph by Deanna Greco (NPS Geologic Resources Division).

Figure 18. Pinnacle Overlook view. This view is to the southwest towards Fern Lake Reservoir. Note the presence of disturbed lands from coal mining activities on the neighboring slopes. National Park Service photograph by Lisa Norby (NPS Geologic Resources Division).

Figure 19. Restored Gap. After two side-by-side tunnels opened in 1996, the park restored the 5.1 km (3.2 mi) of the Wilderness Road across the gap to its historic 1700s location and appearance. Now park visitors can relive the journey through the gap that so many Americans took throughout the 18th and 19th centuries. Photograph by Scott Teodorski (Cumberland Gap National Historical Park).

Geologic Features and Processes

This section describes the most prominent and distinctive geologic features and processes in Cumberland Gap National Historical Park.

Geology and History Connections

The geology of the Cumberland Gap area figures prominently as a framework upon which events of cultural history occur. Developing and presenting connections between geology and human history helps the public to understand the importance of geology in their lives (Whisonant 2002). Luckett (1964) provides an overview of the human history of Cumberland Gap National Historical Park.

Early Exploration and Travel through the Gap

The most tangible geologic connection within the park is Cumberland Gap itself. Ridges of the central Appalachians, such as Cumberland Mountain and Pine Mountain, have long served as barriers to transportation (Andrews 1998). Cumberland Gap, Cumberland Ford Gap, and Pound Gap to the north were major features on the Wilderness Road and other transportation corridors for early explorers, American Indians, settlers, traders, and soldiers (Andrews 1998). Formation of Cumberland Gap via enhanced weathering along a fractured zone (the Rocky Face fault) perpendicular to the ridge of Cumberland Mountain, as described in "Geologic History" below, was a defining process in geologic history that greatly influenced the history of the Cumberland Gap area.

Migrating animals in search of pasture and salt licks (naturally formed evaporite deposits, commonly formed during sea level drops in restricted or closed basins) were likely the first to take advantage of the natural break in the steep ridge of the Appalachian Mountains (Krakow 1987). American Indians (Shawnee, Cherokee, and other eastern woodland tribes) followed the game and later used the gap for trading excursions and as a strategic path during times of war (Krakow 1987). The "Warriors Path" connected the Ohio River valley with the Carolinas and points east directly through Cumberland Gap (Luckett 1964).

Other geologic features in the area guided travelers through the Cumberland Gap area. Atop Cumberland Mountain is Pinnacle Overlook. The pinnacle is a large rock spire that served as an important landmark for early travelers. It is a remnant of a much larger body of rock broken apart by frost-wedging, as evidenced by the fallen blocks littering the surrounding area. Rocks exposed there are Pennsylvanian-aged sandstone (geologic map unit Mpo). The White Rocks also served as an important landmark. White Rocks is a geologic formation of resistant Pennsylvanian sandstone cliffs (geologic map unit PNwpw) that towers 1,100 m (3,500 ft) above Powell Valley, forming a prominent landmark (fig. 20). During the early migrations through Cumberland Gap, the sight of the white cliffs provided westward travelers the indication that they were only a day's journey away from the gap crossing (Thornberry-Ehrlich 2008). Today, visitors can hike the nearly 5 km (3 mi) to the top of White Rocks from the Ewing Trail.

In 1750, Dr. Thomas Walker first mapped the location of the gap. He continued through the Cumberland Ford gap into Kentucky to explore the Cumberland River drainage (Andrews 1998). As described in several diary entries, Walker's party burned Kentucky coal, obtained from exposures of coal beds, in their campfires. This was the first record of the use of coal in the Commonwealth of Kentucky (Andrews 1998). Extensive coal beds are mapped in the park area, see Map Unit Properties Table and Geologic Map Overview Graphics). Later, Daniel Boone marked out what would later become the Wilderness Road through Cumberland Gap (fig. 6).

Indian Rock, an isolated boulder lodged in the path of the gap (likely the result of rockfall), contains scratches and graffiti from settlers passing through. At the height of westward migration through Cumberland Gap, there were likely dozens of trails from different directions traversing through the gap. Today there are no known original segments of these routes (Krakow 1987; Thornberry-Ehrlich 2008). West of the gap, the Middlesboro area served as a stopover for settlers. Its lowland location provided abundant water for travelers, but in poorly drained areas was also subject to marshy conditions that hindered travel (Milam et al. 2005).

Industry

Underlying geologic structures and bedrock support different natural resource opportunities on either side of the gap. Local industry focused on geologic resources, in particular the abundant coal and iron ore resources (Whisonant 2002). The gap allowed for the transportation of manufactured products between east and west thereby promoting the local economy.

Historic mine features inside the park occur along the Greenleaf trail, Chadwell Gap, and Honey Tree spur loop. At Chadwell Gap, the mine opening and the associated coke ovens were the subject of a special interpretive hike in 2010 as well as a local cable program. The opening and ovens are accessible to visitors, but the opening is blocked by metal bars to prevent entry into the mine. The park plans to install an interpretive wayside exhibit at the coke oven location. Remnants of a large haul system exist at the Chadwell Gap mine. On the Greenleaf and Honey Tree spur loop, the mine features are not interpreted or obvious to visitors (J. Beeler, resource management specialist, Cumberland Gap NHP, written communication, January 2011). Local miners also extracted potassium nitrate (saltpeter or "nitre") from sediments in small caves and shelters in the area. Saltpeter is an oxidizing component that when combined with charcoal and sulfur "brimstone" makes black powder. Mining for saltpeter from mines near Cumberland Gap peaked before the American Civil War. Historic remnants from saltpeter and other mining activity are present in several gated caves, including remains of vats, hewn wood troughs, mortised timber remnants, a short ladder, burnt lightwood and pine torches, stoneware fragments, excavated earth, and log bridges across drops. Historic graffiti in the caves includes dates from 1854 through 1941. Some remnants, such as the ladder, are part of the park's historic collection. However, the park currently has no plans to interpret these features as they are difficult to access (J. Beeler, resource management specialist, Cumberland Gap NHP, written communication, January 2011).

Strategic Importance during the Civil War

During the American Civil War, both the Confederate and Union armies recognized the strategic importance of Cumberland Gap as a transportation corridor between the border state of Kentucky and Tennessee. Control of the gap meant control of a vital railway between Virginia and Tennessee. It changed hands several times throughout the war (Luckett 1964; Thornberry-Ehrlich 2008). Prior to the Battle of Perryville (Kentucky) on October 8, 1862 in central Kentucky, Cumberland Gap provided an easily accessible route into central Kentucky for Confederate forces.

As an aside, geologic processes contributed to the tactics of the Battle of Perryville. Ordovician-aged carbonate rocks of the Chickamauga Group underlie the battlefield and surrounding area. The resultant karst terrain lacks abundant surface water (streams, etc). Kentucky was in a deep drought at the time, making the already rare surface water resources particularly valuable. Both armies recognized this importance and fought, in part, to protect access to the limited water resources (Gregory et al. 1999). The Battle of Perryville, the largest Civil War battle fought in Kentucky, ended Confederate hopes of occupying Kentucky, and they retreated back, across Cumberland Gap into Tennessee (Andrews 2004).

The area that is now Pinnacle Overlook served not only as an important landmark for early travelers but also another area of strategically high ground during the Civil War (Milam et al. 2005). Both armies used the Pinnacle area as a vantage point while guarding Cumberland Gap. The armies clear-cut trees on the surrounding ridges to provide better strategic views; a situation which likely accelerated local erosion. These slopes have since naturally revegetated.

In September 1862, following an unsuccessful attempt to stop 12,000 Confederates from crossing into Kentucky, Morgan retreated, destroying the commissary and ammunition stores in a great explosion which could be seen for many miles. Today, the scar is visible along the trail to Tri-State Peak (fig. 21). Confederates then refortified and occupied the area until the final Union capture in September of 1863. Military fortifications at Cumberland Gap were abandoned for the last time in 1866.

From Post War Isolation to Transportation Corridor

After the Civil War, the geology of the area served to isolate the Cumberland Gap coal field from extensive survey and commercial development until the early 1900's. Wilderness Road was largely abandoned at this time. Ashley (1904) describes the area as hedged in by high mountain ridges with Pine Mountain to the west, "so steep that for miles not even a wagon road crosses it". Cumberland and Black Mountains to the east and north and Fork Mountain to the southwest close in the area. The town of Middlesboro, Kentucky was planned ahead of a predicted industrial boom. Due to a lack of railroad following the Civil War, the boom did not materialize (Ashley 1904). The transportation system was eventually built to handle the industrial potential and coal reserves within the Cumberland Gap coal field (Ashley 1904). Gaps through the ridges of central Appalachia still provide important thoroughfares for highways and railways. More recently, U.S. 23, completed in 1998, goes through Pound Gap of Pine Mountain, exposing a nearly continuous section of Mississippian-aged strata (Andrews 1998).

Tools for Interpreting Historic Connections to Geology

The Southeastern Maps and Aerial Photographic Systems project in Tennessee uses specially selected and compiled satellite and aerial imagery, topographic maps, and special-purpose cartographic products to create 3D anaglyph maps for hands-on instructional and interpretive tools. These maps provide a stereoscopic 3D effect, made up of two superimposed color layers, offset with respect to each other to produce a depth effect when viewed with special glasses. For Cumberland Gap, the project explores connections among the geology, early European settlement, highway tunnel geological engineering, and problems of landscape origins (Clark et al. 2000). This type of derivative product is a valuable tool for interpretation at Cumberland Gap National Historical Park tying geology to the history of the area and the subsequent development of the landscape.

Paleontological Resources

Paleontological resources are any remains of past life preserved in a geologic context. Paleontological resources include body fossils (e.g. shells, bones, teeth, leaves) and trace fossils (e.g. burrows, coprolites, footprints). These non-renewable resources possess great scientific, educational, and interpretive value. Fossil resources at Cumberland Gap National Historical Park have yet to be comprehensively inventoried in the field (Thornberry-Ehrlich 2008). Hunt-Foster et al. (2009) presents a thorough literature-based review of fossils known to be within the bedrock units exposed in the park as well as fossils that might be exposed in the park.

The Mississippian and Pennsylvanian units throughout the park contain abundant marine fossils including colonial corals, in addition to *Lepidodendron* tree trunks and other plant remains. The Upper Mississippian Newman Limestone, exposed in the southwestern portion of the park in Virginia and Tennessee, contains crinoids, blastoids, conodonts, and worm tubes (Ettensohn and Bliefnick 1982; Hunt-Foster et al. 2009). During the excavation of the Cumberland Gap Tunnel, fossil remains uncovered included a few unidentified plant and animal fossils from the Newman Limestone and the overlying Pennington and Breathitt groups (Santucci et al. 2001). The sandstone- and shale-rich formations of the Upper Mississippian-Lower Pennsylvanian Pennington Group, though easily eroded and often covered, contain crinoids, blastoids, conodonts, spores, and burrows (Greb 2006; Ettensohn and Bliefnick 1982). The cliff-forming, conglomeratic sandstones of the Pennsylvanian Breathitt Group contain scant fossil plants (Hunt-Foster et al. 2009). See the Map Unit Properties Table for more information. The Geologic History section contains additional descriptions about ancient environments of the area.

Geologic features such as caves, karst traps (collapsed sinkholes), notches, and alcoves may contain vertebrate fossil remains dating back to the Pleistocene. Pleistocene fossil remains in the park include a partially articulated, poorly preserved black bear (*Ursus americanus*) skeleton found by The Cave Research Foundation in Gap Cave.

Santucci et al. (2009) presented five "vital signs" and suggested monitoring methodologies for paleontological resources: erosion (geologic and climatic factors); catastrophic geohazards; hydrology/bathymetry; and human access/public use. Rates of natural erosion are influenced by the physical characteristics of the bedrock, bedding, degree of slope, and geochemistry, as well as climatic factors such as precipitation and temperature. The stability of in situ fossils is proportional to the erosion rates of the units in which they are preserved. Geohazards which may affect paleontological resources include volcanism, geothermal activity, earthquakes, glacial activity, and mass wasting events such as landslides. For fossils occurring in areas submerged by or adjacent to marine or freshwater, knowledge of the water levels and associated hydrologic processes will aid in understanding how paleontological resources will respond to changes in the hydrologic regime. Human activities such as agriculture, mining, forestry, oil and gas development, and the use of all-terrain vehicles may negatively impact fossil resources.

Middlesboro Meteorite Impact Structure

Middlesboro, Kentucky is located within a circular basin created by a meteorite impact. Although not located within Cumberland Gap National Historical Park boundaries, the structure is easily visible from the park. Morning fog often settles into the circular structure making it especially evident from Pinnacle Overlook and other vantage points within the park (cover and fig. 1). The structure is plainly visible on the geologic map (Geologic Map Overview Graphics).

Rich (1933) was unable to come up with a satisfactory structural geology explanation for the existence of what was termed the "Middlesboro basin." The origin of the structure remained enigmatic until the 1960s when geologic mapping revealed the presence of intensely deformed bedrock, normal faulting with circular trends around the basin, overturned beds, "shattered" quartz grains, and a central core of uplifted material—all considered evidence of impact from a meteorite or other cosmic material (Milam et al. 2005). Circular faults and fractures form outer and inner rings, defining the extent of the meteorite impact structure (Geologic Map Overview Graphic). The center of the structure features a small, uplifted area that formed as a "pop-up" during the impact. Pop-ups form much like a rebounding drop of water into a puddle; they are masses of rock uplifted by reverse slip on two or more faults that dip toward a common point beneath the mass.

Today, homes in Middlesboro cover this small hill. Within the impact structure itself, the original rock units are pervasively deformed and fractured (fig. 22). They are mapped as intensely deformed equivalents of bedrock units (geologic map units PNbd, PNbdc2, PNbdss, and PNbdc1) (Sparks and Lambert 2003). Further evidence of an impact-related origin can be found in the textures of the rock. Rock textures within the Middlesboro basin include shocked quartz grains (microscopic features indicative of rapid deformation under very high pressure), chaotic rock breccias (angular, "broken" clasts in a finer-grained matrix), and cone-in-cone structures (thin shale layers that resemble a set of nested cones). Due to this extensive deformation, the rocks within the structure are nearly unconsolidated and especially susceptible to erosion where disturbed by anthropogenic activity (Milam et al. 2005; Thornberry-Ehrlich 2008).

Interestingly, the rocks visible at the surface today were originally 300 m (1,000 ft) below the crater. Over time, erosion removed the overlying rocks exposing rocks that were deformed far below the actual impact surface. Mass wasting, slope creep, slumps, and landslides present serious geohazard issues for urban development within the impact structure, especially in areas near the edges of the structure where developers dig into steep slopes (Milam et al. 2005). If the boundaries Cumberland Gap National Historical Park were ever to expand westward into the extent of the impact structure, these types of slope issues would be a concern for resource managers.

There is still debate as to when the meteorite impact took place. Given its position in the midst of a down-warped fold, called a syncline, associated with the Alleghany Orogeny period of Appalachian Mountain-building, the structure likely post dates Appalachian Mountain building (Milam et al. 2005). See the "Geologic History" section for more information.

Excellent Rock Exposures

Though not formal type sections (a particular outcrop of rock or sequence of strata where a geologic unit was originally described), there are excellent exposures of Mississippian and Pennsylvanian units (including geologic map units Mpo, PNwp, PNah, and PNsw) within Cumberland Gap National Historical Park. Many of these contributed greatly to the understanding of the stratigraphy and structure of the central Appalachian basin (Dean 1989; Englund et al. 1994). Such exposures include White Rocks, Devils Garden, the Pinnacle Overlook area, and the trail to Tri-State Peak. The black shales of the Devonian-Mississippian Chattanooga Shale (geologic map unit MDc) outcrops at the lowest elevations in the area. Some local geologic units contain carbonate intergranular cements or entire beds of carbonates such as limestone and dolomite including the Newman Limestone (geologic units Mn, Mnl, Mnu). Other notable rock exposures include the Pennington Group (Pinnacle Overlook Sandstone, geologic map unit Mpo). Geologists use the excellent exposures to describe, name, and group rocks in the area. However, different naming schemes and interpretations by different geologic mappers have lead to different names for the same rocks (fig. 26). The names and definitions of geologic units differ locally across state boundaries. The U.S. Geological Survey maintains a website pertaining to the descriptions and locations of type sections across the United States: http://ngmdb.usgs.gov/Geolex/.

Significant Features

Noteworthy geologic features within Cumberland Gap National Historical Park and surrounding areas under NPS legislation include waterfalls, "proto-arches" (weathered fins of rock in the process of forming an open arch), Devil's Garden, Pinnacle Overlook, and peat bogs. Isolated, small-scale arches may be present in remote areas.

Steep slopes and pervasive, resistant sandstone ledges create waterfalls on streams draining both sides of the park's ridges. Resistant sandstones also tend to become isolated when neighboring, less resistant layers weather away leaving prominent fins, rock shelters, and potentially, arches (Thornberry-Ehrlich 2008).

On the northwestern flank of Cumberland Mountain, below Gibson Gap, Devil's Garden is a large boulder field formed by frost-wedging of Pennsylvanian conglomeratic rocks (Sewanee Sandstone, geologic map unit PNss) along similarly-oriented groups of fractures within the rocks. Melt water from snow and rain trickles through cracks in the rock and freezes at night during the colder months. The expansion of the ice in the cracks enhances action by tree and plant roots to wedge the rocks apart. Often slope creep processes slowly move the rocks away, separating them into masses of interesting configurations (Thornberry-Ehrlich 2008).

Along the Martins Fork drainage, on either side of the creek, is the largest peat bog known to exist in the state of Kentucky. The underlying geologic framework of bedrock and structure influenced the location of this and other upland bogs within the park. Units such as the Pennington Group (geologic map unit Mp) are prone to forming broad ridges and swales (Kentucky Geological Survey staff, written communication, 2008) that form foundations for some broad reaches along the streams conducive to bog development. Long-standing sites of deposition, peat bogs commonly contain paleoclimate information including pollen and plant remains from thousands of years ago. Decaying plant remains in upland bogs may also contribute to a lower pH in the Martins Fork drainage (Thornberry-Ehrlich 2008).

Figure 20. White Rocks. The "White Rocks" of the park are composed of Warren Point Sandstone (White Rocks sandstone bed, map unit PNwpw). The prominent cliffs were used as orientation points for early migrations through the area. Rock climbing in the area may impact the cliffs themselves as well as the surrounding vegetation (including an endangered species, as described in the Geologic Issues section). National Park Service photographs.

Figure 21. Civil War crater. This small crater along the trail to Tri-State Peak was formed by exploding munitions during the Union retreat from Cumberland Gap during the American Civil War. Photograph by Trista L. Thornberry-Ehrlich (Colorado State University).

Figure 22. Impact structure. This exposure near Middlesboro shows the intensely fractured rocks within the Middlesboro meteorite impact structure. Note the presence of talus at the base of the slope; brecciated units are prone to mass wasting in the area. Photograph by Lisa Norby (NPS Geologic Resources Division).

Geologic History

This section describes the rocks and unconsolidated deposits that appear on the digital geologic map of Cumberland Gap National Historical Park, the environment in which those units were deposited, and the timing of geologic events that formed the present landscape.

The geologic history of Cumberland Gap National Historical Park records a long portion of Earth's geologic history, from the Cambrian Period (approximately 580 million years ago) to the Late Pennsylvanian (approximately 300 million years ago) with a much less continuous record to the present day's unconsolidated surficial geologic units (figs. 23 and 26). These features represent a wide variety of depositional environments and dynamic processes that shaped today's landscape. The park's folded and deformed rocks attest to many periods of deformation associated with several major Appalachian orogenies (mountain-building events) (figs. 24 and 25).

Precambrian (before 542 million years ago)

During the late Precambrian, most of the continental crust in existence at the time was assembled into a supercontinent called Rodinia during the Grenville Orogeny. The metamorphic granites and gneisses in the core of the modern Blue Ridge Mountains to the north and east of Cumberland Mountain are a result of the sedimentation, deformation, plutonism, and volcanism that created Rodinia (Harris et al. 1997). These metamorphic rocks are more than a billion years old, and following their uplift and exposure to erosion, formed a basement upon which all other rocks of the Appalachians accumulated (Southworth et al. 2001). Approximately 565 million years ago, Rodinia split apart (rifted) into large landmasses called Laurentia, Baltica, Avalonia, and Gondwana. Rocks of Laurentia now form the oldest core of North America, Baltica's rocks now underlie much of eastern Eurasia, while rocks of Avalonia can now be found in south-west Great Britain and the east coast of North America. The rocks of Gondwana would later become Antarctica, South America, Africa, Madagascar, Australia-New Guinea, New Zealand, Arabia and India. This rifting opened a series of marine basins culminating in the Iapetus Ocean; the predecessor to today's Atlantic Ocean basin. Sediments began collecting in the basin off the eastern edge of Laurentia (Milam et al. 2005).

Cambrian Period (about 532–488 million years ago)

The oldest rocks included in the park's digital geologic (GIS) data are thin-bedded red shales, siltstone, and sandstone of the Rome Formation (geologic map unit Cr; Geologic Map Overview Graphic; Map Unit Properties Table). The sediments making up the Rome Formation rocks were originally deposited in the Iapetus Ocean in shallow marine and nearshore terrestrial environments (Harris et al. 1962; Milam et al. 2005). The shales of this unit would play a later role in the development of the Pine Mountain thrust sheet (see "Permian Period" below). Deposited on top of the Rome Formation are the rocks of the Conasauga Group that include mixed shales, limestones, and dolomite of the Pumpkin Valley Shale (Cpv), Rutledge Limestone (Crt), Rogersville Shale (Crg), Maryville Limestone (Cm), Conasauga Shale (Cc), Maynardsville Limestone (Cmn), and Copper Ridge Dolomite (Ccr) (Harris et al. 1962). Shales tend to dominate the lower units of the Conasauga Group becoming more limestone-rich towards the top. This transition accompanied the formation of a stable carbonate platform along the eastern margin of Laurentia that persisted from the Late Cambrian through Early Ordovician (Harris et al. 1962; Milam et al. 2005).

Ordovician Period (about 488–444 million years ago)

The stable carbonate platform which existed at the end of the Cambrian persisted into the Ordovician and is indicative of warm, shallow marine conditions like today's Bahamas. Carbonate rocks (dolomites and limestones) of the Knox Group were part of this platform off the eastern coast of Laurentia (fig. 24) (Milam et al. 2005). The Knox Group includes the Chepultepec Dolomite (Oc, Ocu, Ocl), Mascot Dolomite (Oma), Kingsport Formation (Ok), Longview Dolomite (Ol), and Newala Dolomite (On).

During the Middle Ordovician Taconic Orogeny, a volcanic island arc collided with and accreted onto the eastern margin of Laurentia during the first of the major Appalachian Mountain-building events (figs. 24 and 25) (Milam et al. 2005). Deposition in the park area was interrupted at this time and rocks from the Middle Ordovician are not contained in the rock record. During the Upper Ordovician, marine deposition resumed as evidenced by the mixed gray shales, limestones, and dolomites of the Chickamauga Group. These are the oldest rocks mapped within park boundaries (see Map Unit Properties Table). At the end of the Ordovician, interlayered marine sediments that would later become siltstone, shale, limestone, and some sandstone of the Sequatchie Formation (Os) were deposited atop the Chickamauga Group (Englund et al. 1963).

Silurian Period (about 444–416 million years ago)

Deposition within the basin continued into the Silurian with coarse sandstone and interlayered shale and siltstone of the Clinch Sandstone (Sc) forming above the Ordovician Sequatchie Formation (Englund et al. 1963). Distal storm shelf depositional environments were the setting for the formation of geologic units such as the thin-bedded sandstone and shale facies interlayered with thin-bedded limestone of the Rockwood Formation (Sr) (Driese 1988). These rocks are visible in roadcuts along U.S. Highway 25E and are stratigraphically above calcareous, silty red beds of Upper Ordovician age (Sequatchie Formation [Os]) (Englund 1964; Driese 1988). Crossbeds preserved within the Rockwood Formation at Cumberland Gap indicate waves arriving from the northwest, whereas flute and groove measurements show directions in northeast-southwest directed wave energy (Driese 1988). These two lines of evidence suggest the presence of changing paleocurrents during the deposition of the Rockwood. "Tempestites" within this unit indicate deposition during storm events (Driese 1988).

Shifting depositional environments within the basin continued with the formation of the Clinton Shale (Sct). This unit includes shale deposited in relatively calm water interlayered with siltstone and some fine- to medium-grained sandstone which can indicate higher energy, nearshore conditions (source Harris et al. 1962) or potentially submarine avalanche deposits (turbidites). The Hancock Dolomite (Sh) contains coral reef zones and some sandstone lenses indicative of nearshore, fringing environments within the basin (source Englund 1964).

Devonian Period (416–359 million years ago)

During the Devonian, Laurentia collided with at least one microcontinent during an event called the Acadian Orogeny (figs. 24 and 25) (Milam et al. 2005). Effects of this orogeny were focused further east and north of the Cumberland Gap area where the thin-bedded, pyritic, black shale of the Chattanooga Shale (MDc) accumulated in an open basin (fig. 25A). This formation would later play a role in the formation of the Pine Mountain thrust sheet (see "Permian Period" below). As early as Late Devonian time, intermittent periods of sea level retreat (regression) and advance (transgression) meant that depositional environments alternated between terrestrial and marine (Englund et al. 1994). Transgressive periods are marked by dark shales, whereas thin, laterally extensive grayish siltstones and sandstones were deposited during regressive periods (Filer 1998).

Mississippian through Pennsylvanian Periods (359–299 million years ago)

Throughout the Mississippian, a regional carbonate platform was the primary depositional environment for rocks exposed at Cumberland Gap National Historical Park (fig. 24). From the Late Mississippian to Early Pennsylvanian, nearly 760 m (2,500 ft) of interlayered limestone, shale, sandstone (with minor amounts of siltstone), claystone, and coal collected in the Appalachian basin (Englund et al. 1994). From oldest to youngest, these are the Newman Limestone, Pennington Group, and Breathitt Group (many geologic map units are encompassed by these groups, refer to Map Unit Properties Table and Geologic Map Overview Graphics). These assemblages of rock form the majority of the exposures along Cumberland Mountain, particularly near the gap. Periodically, vast marsh and swamp areas developed in the Appalachian Basin. These areas collected vast amounts of organic deposits that eventually developed into commercially viable and culturally significant coal seams in the park area (e.g. PNahst, PNbrc1, PNgcf) (Englund et al. 1964).

Regionally, deposition of the thick lower members of the Newman Limestone (Mnl) represents the most widespread marine incursion. An intermittent regression in Late Mississippian time deposited thin coal beds (between units Mnu and Mnl), possibly in coastal marsh environments in the middle reaches of the Newman Limestone interrupting the episode of open marine conditions. Shale interbedded with limestone, siltstone, and sandstone in the upper portions of the Newman Limestone record a return of marine conditions before deposition of the Pennington Group (Englund et al. 1994).

At the end of the Mississippian, deposition included a shale and sandstone unit followed by a resistant, pure quartz sandstone with units exhibiting ripple marks (the lower members of the Pennington Group (Mpl, Mpo, and Mpu)). The Pennington Group also contains coal beds as much as 76 cm (30 in.) thick. This coarse sandstone with interbedded coal indicates regressive (sea level fall) trends as the open marine conditions changed to nearshore or even terrestrial depositional environments (fig. 25B) (Englund et al. 1994). The Pinnacle Overlook Sandstone (Mpo) is a partly conglomeratic, relatively pure sandstone that grades laterally into siltstone and shale (Kohl and Sykes 1991; Englund et al. 1994). The upper layers of the Pennington Group contain shale interbedded with thin beds of fossiliferous limestone, sandstone, and coal indicating a variety of shifting depositional environments from nearshore marshes to open marine basins (Englund et al. 1963; Englund et al. 1994).

The nature of the Mississippian-Pennsylvanian boundary in the Cumberland Mountain region is the subject of some confusion. Pennsylvanian sandstones appear to interfinger with Upper Mississippian sandstones and much debate centers around the nomenclature and timing of deformation and deposition of these units (Watson and Ettensohn 1991). In addition, although Paleozoic strata of the Appalachian basin generally increase in thickness southeastward (Englund et al. 1994), Upper Mississippian and Lower Pennsylvanian strata do not correlate between the portals of the Cumberland Gap Tunnel on the east and west sides of Cumberland Mountain. The lack of correlation in the tunnel is due to left-lateral displacement along the Rocky Face fault, meaning that rocks across the fault appear to have been moved to the left. The Rocky Face fault trends perpendicular to the orientation of the Pine Mountain thrust sheet trace and runs directly through Cumberland Gap. Displacement along this fault is at least 2.4 km (1.5 mi) and juxtaposes contrasting stratigraphic sections across the fault. Deformation associated with the Rocky

Face Fault may have had some structural control during the deposition of the sandstone units (Watson and Ettensohn 1991). The Pinnacle Overlook member of the Pennington Formation sits directly beneath Pennsylvanian sandstones of the Warren Point Sandstone on the northeast side of the fault, whereas on the southwest side of the fault, a series of Pennington shales sits between the two sandstones. The Warren Point Sandstone was formerly the Chadwell member of the Lee Formation [see fig. 26]. This configuration may indicate potential early Pennsylvanian uplift along the Rocky Face fault prior to the next major mountain building event (Watson and Ettensohn 1991; Chestnut 1992).

At the end of the Pennsylvanian, collisional tectonics of the Allegheny Orogeny began again along the eastern margin of North America as the African landmass approached. It resulted in the formation of a single supercontinent, Pangaea, and was the final stage in forming the Appalachian Mountains (Milam et al. 2005). The Alleghany Orogeny was a pervasive event of deformation and mountain building in the Cumberland Gap area. The Pine Mountain thrust sheet and Rocky Face faults were active at this time.

Permian Period (299–251 million years ago)

Rocks of Permian age do not crop out on the surface at Cumberland Gap National Historical Park. If ever deposited, they have long since eroded from the landscape. However, tectonic events during the Late Pennsylvanian and early Permian had profound effects on the landscape at the park. The Pine Mountain thrust sheet formation occurred during the Alleghany Orogeny (figs. 24 and 25C) (Dean 1989). The sheet is one of a series of major thrusts that characterize the fold-thrust belt of the Southern Appalachians. Thrust sheets are immense bodies of rock that were shoved up and over other rocks during mountain building events. There are two horizons, separated by 2,100 m (7,000 ft) along which rocks fractured, detached, and moved in the park area. The lower horizon formed in shaley layers near the base of the Lower Cambrian Rome Formation (see cross section, fig. 5) (Dean 1989). The upper horizon lies near the base of the Upper Devonian Chattanooga Shale (Dean 1989). The thrust fault ramps up between these two surfaces and then again ramps up to the surface where it can be traced at the base of Pine Mountain. The first ramp is responsible for the formation of the Middlesboro Syncline-Powell Valley Anticline structure and the second ramp formed Pine Mountain (fig. 25D). The tilted rock layers visible at Cumberland Mountain trace the angle of the ramp occurring in the hanging wall of the Pine Mountain thrust fault. Cumberland Mountain is the eroded remnant of the "nose" or leading edge of the thrusted rock units (Dean 1989).

Mesozoic Era (251–65.5 million years ago)

At the end of the Paleozoic Era, the Appalachian Mountains had formed and all of Earth's continental crust sutured together into one large supercontinent, called Pangaea (fig. 24). The Middlesboro Syncline, Powell Valley Anticline, Doublings fault zone, Rocky Face fault, and Pine Mountain thrust sheet had already formed at this time as products of compressive forces associated with Appalachian Mountain building. The compressive forces ceased and eventually, Pangaea began to pull apart into roughly the continents that persist today. Rift basins formed along the eastern margin of North America. Examples of these basins include the Culpeper and Danville basins of central Virginia. None of these basins are present in the Cumberland Gap area. Without compressive forces pushing the Appalachians higher, erosion became the dominant shaper of the topography (Milam et al. 2005).

Erosion and weathering preferentially removed less resistant types of rock such as shale forming depressions and left more resistant rocks such as sandstone behind as ridges. This preferential removal of less resistant rock caused the Powell Valley Anticline to appear as a topographic low, floored by limestone and dolomite units. Conversely the Middlesboro Syncline appears as a dissected upland underlain by more resistant Pennsylvanian sandstone units (fig. 25F).

The location and development of Cumberland Gap was long considered a topographic problem because it existed hundreds of feet above a viable water drainage presumed to have carved it (Davis 1915). Now it is widely accepted that the Rocky Face Fault is responsible for the location and formation of the Cumberland Gap. The Rocky Face Fault developed during Appalachian mountain building. By virtue of fracturing and displacing rocks, the fault was a zone of weaker rocks that were more susceptible to erosion than adjacent non faulted rocks. Weathering and erosion exploited this weaker zone, creating a "gap." Note the trace of the Rocky Face fault passing through the gap (fig. 5 and Geologic Map Overview Graphics). The offset of geologic units on either side of the fault is also apparent.

Cenozoic Era (the past 65.5 million years)

The primary geologic story of the Cenozoic Era for Cumberland Gap National Historical Park is erosion and removal of rock, exposing underlying geologic structures and rock units. Glaciers from the Pleistocene ice ages never reached Cumberland Mountain, but the colder climates of the ice ages played a role in the formation of the landscape. The higher ridges in the area experienced periglacial conditions that included many freeze-thaw cycles. Freeze-thaw cycles and subsequent ice-wedging, led to the formation of thousands of boulders and smaller rocks from the ridge tops. Ice would melt during the day and meltwater would seep into cracks, freeze at night, expand, and force the rocks apart. The resultant material was transported downslope creating talus piles. The periglacial conditions that existed at higher altitudes also intensified weathering and other erosional processes, yielding higher sediment loads in local streams and rivers (Harris et al. 1997).

Today, erosion and mass wasting continue within the park. Landslide deposits (Qls) attest to active mass wasting and colluvium (Ql) mantles the bases of many if not all steep slopes within the park (Rice and Maughan 1978). Streams are actively incising channels along the length of Cumberland Mountain's ridge. Stream terraces of sand, silt, clay, boulders, and gravel (Qt units) are deposited along these streams, perched above normal flood levels (Englund 1964; Rice and Maughan 1978). Underfit streams incising floodplains are a common feature suggesting the drainage had far greater capacity to move sediment in the past than in recent times. Spilling from the mouths of deep ravines notched in the mountainside are mixed boulders, gravel, sand, and silt of alluvial fan deposits (Qaf) (Maughan and Tazelaar 1973). Within the streams, well sorted sand, silt, clay, and gravel line the channels as alluvium (Qal) (Englund 1964; Maughan and Tazelaar 1973). Boulders within these streams can reach dramatic proportions with individual boulders as large as busses in Shillalah Creek (fig. 8).

Anthropogenic activities continue to alter the landscape at Cumberland Gap National Historical Park. Artificial fill used to stabilize eroding slopes or compose stabilizing engineered structures appears on the digital geologic map for the park (Qf) (Kohl and Sykes 1991). Other activities, such as road and tunnel construction, trail restoration and use, visitor facility development and maintenance, and stream diversion altered the park's natural landscape. Surface coal mining in the surrounding areas illustrates the regions continued utilization of the rich natural resources—the products of hundreds of millions of years of geologic history.

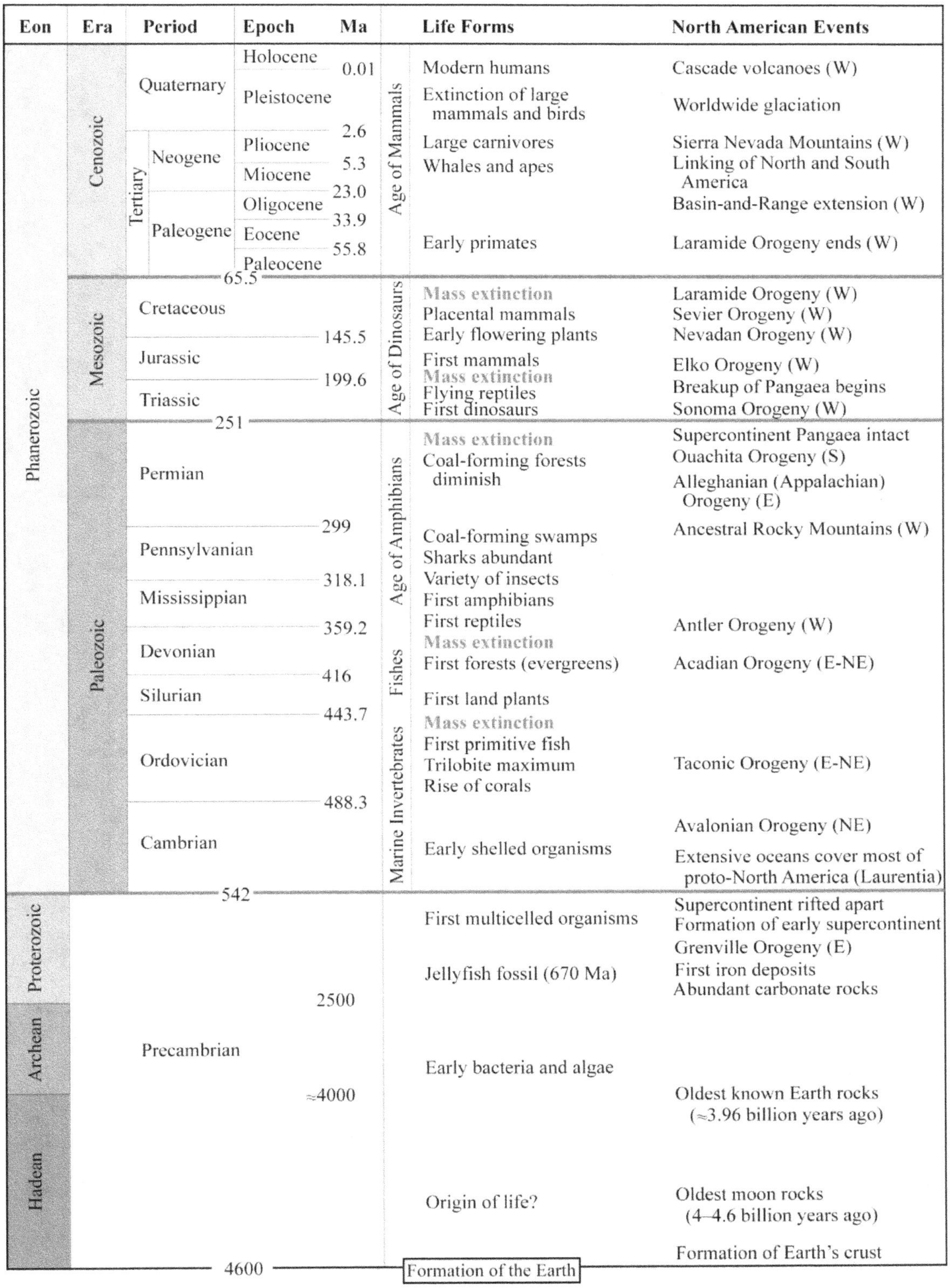

Eon	Era	Period	Epoch	Ma		Life Forms	North American Events
Phanerozoic	Cenozoic	Quaternary	Holocene	0.01	Age of Mammals	Modern humans	Cascade volcanoes (W)
			Pleistocene	2.6		Extinction of large mammals and birds	Worldwide glaciation
		Tertiary – Neogene	Pliocene	5.3		Large carnivores	Sierra Nevada Mountains (W)
			Miocene	23.0		Whales and apes	Linking of North and South America
		Tertiary – Paleogene	Oligocene	33.9			Basin-and-Range extension (W)
			Eocene	55.8		Early primates	Laramide Orogeny ends (W)
			Paleocene	65.5			
	Mesozoic	Cretaceous		145.5	Age of Dinosaurs	Mass extinction Placental mammals Early flowering plants	Laramide Orogeny (W) Sevier Orogeny (W) Nevadan Orogeny (W)
		Jurassic		199.6		First mammals Mass extinction	Elko Orogeny (W)
		Triassic		251		Flying reptiles First dinosaurs	Breakup of Pangaea begins Sonoma Orogeny (W)
	Paleozoic	Permian		299	Age of Amphibians	Mass extinction Coal-forming forests diminish	Supercontinent Pangaea intact Ouachita Orogeny (S) Alleghanian (Appalachian) Orogeny (E)
		Pennsylvanian		318.1		Coal-forming swamps Sharks abundant Variety of insects	Ancestral Rocky Mountains (W)
		Mississippian		359.2		First amphibians First reptiles	Antler Orogeny (W)
		Devonian		416	Fishes	Mass extinction First forests (evergreens)	Acadian Orogeny (E-NE)
		Silurian		443.7		First land plants	
		Ordovician		488.3	Marine Invertebrates	Mass extinction First primitive fish Trilobite maximum Rise of corals	Taconic Orogeny (E-NE)
		Cambrian		542		Early shelled organisms	Avalonian Orogeny (NE) Extensive oceans cover most of proto-North America (Laurentia)
Proterozoic		Precambrian		2500		First multicelled organisms Jellyfish fossil (670 Ma)	Supercontinent rifted apart Formation of early supercontinent Grenville Orogeny (E) First iron deposits Abundant carbonate rocks
Archean				≈4000		Early bacteria and algae	Oldest known Earth rocks (≈3.96 billion years ago)
Hadean				4600		Origin of life? Formation of the Earth	Oldest moon rocks (4–4.6 billion years ago) Formation of Earth's crust

Figure 23. Geologic timescale. Included are major life history and tectonic events occurring on the North American continent. Red lines indicate major unconformities between eras. Radiometric ages shown are in millions of years (Ma). Compass directions in parentheses indicate the regional location of individual geologic events. Graphic by Trista L. Thornberry-Erhlich (Colorado State University) with information from the U.S. Geological Survey (http://pubs.usgs.gov/fs/2007/3015/) and the International Commission on Stratigraphy (http://www.stratigraphy.org/view.php?id=25).

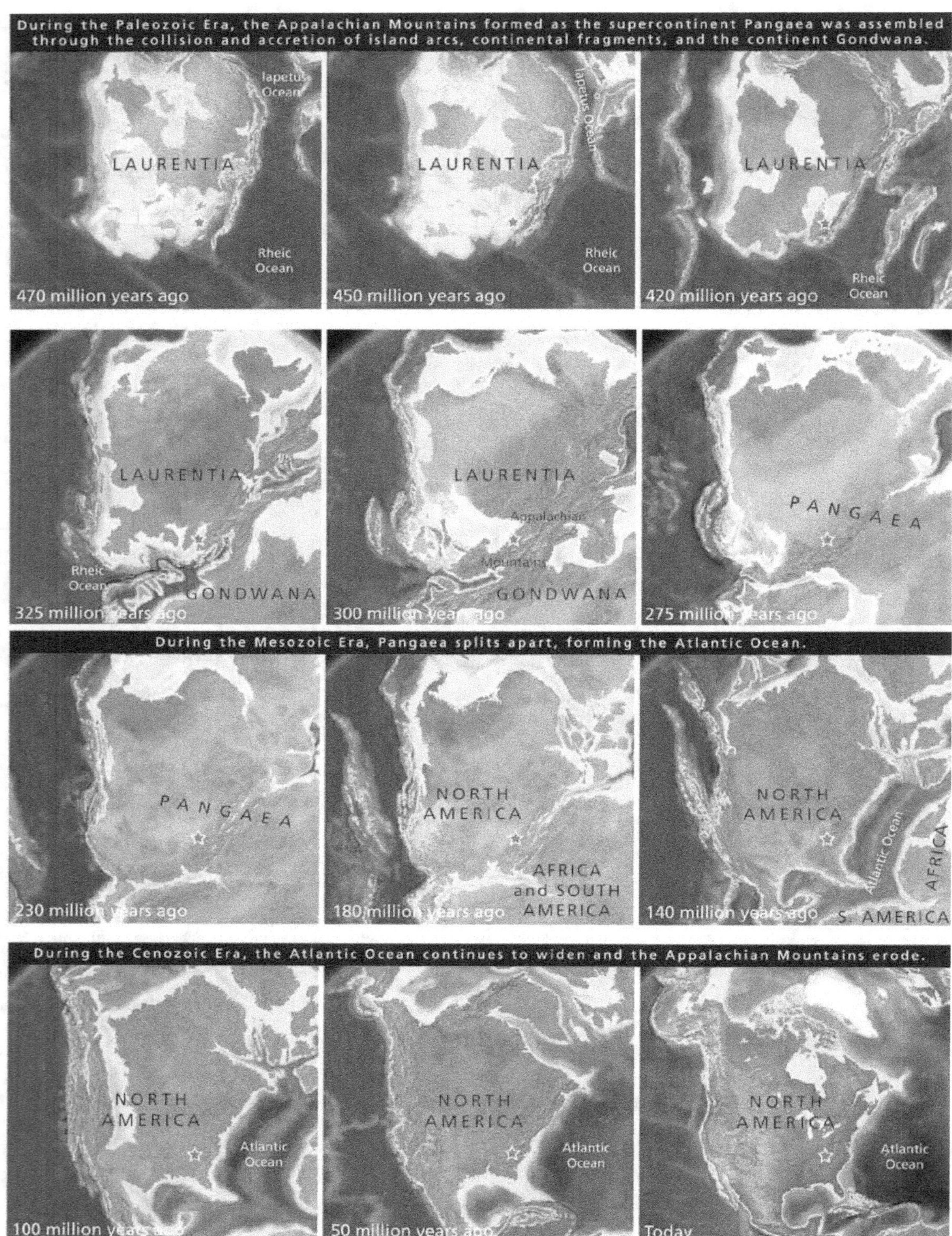

Figure 24. Paleogeography of North America. The bedrock geologic units of Cumberland Gap National Historical Park are tied to the intense deformation and intrusion of molten material as the Appalachian Mountains formed during several Paleozoic orogenies. These orogenies lead to the assembly of the supercontinent Pangaea. Pangaea began to split apart during the Mesozoic and the Appalachian Mountains began to erode. Today, the Atlantic Ocean continues to widen and erosion has exposed the core of the Appalachian Mountains. Red stars indicate approximate location of Cumberland Gap National Historical Park. Graphic compiled and annotated by Jason Kenworthy (NPS Geologic Resources Division). Base paleogeographic maps by Ron Blakey (Colorado Plateau Geosystems, Inc.) and available online: http://cpgeosystems.com/paleomaps.html.

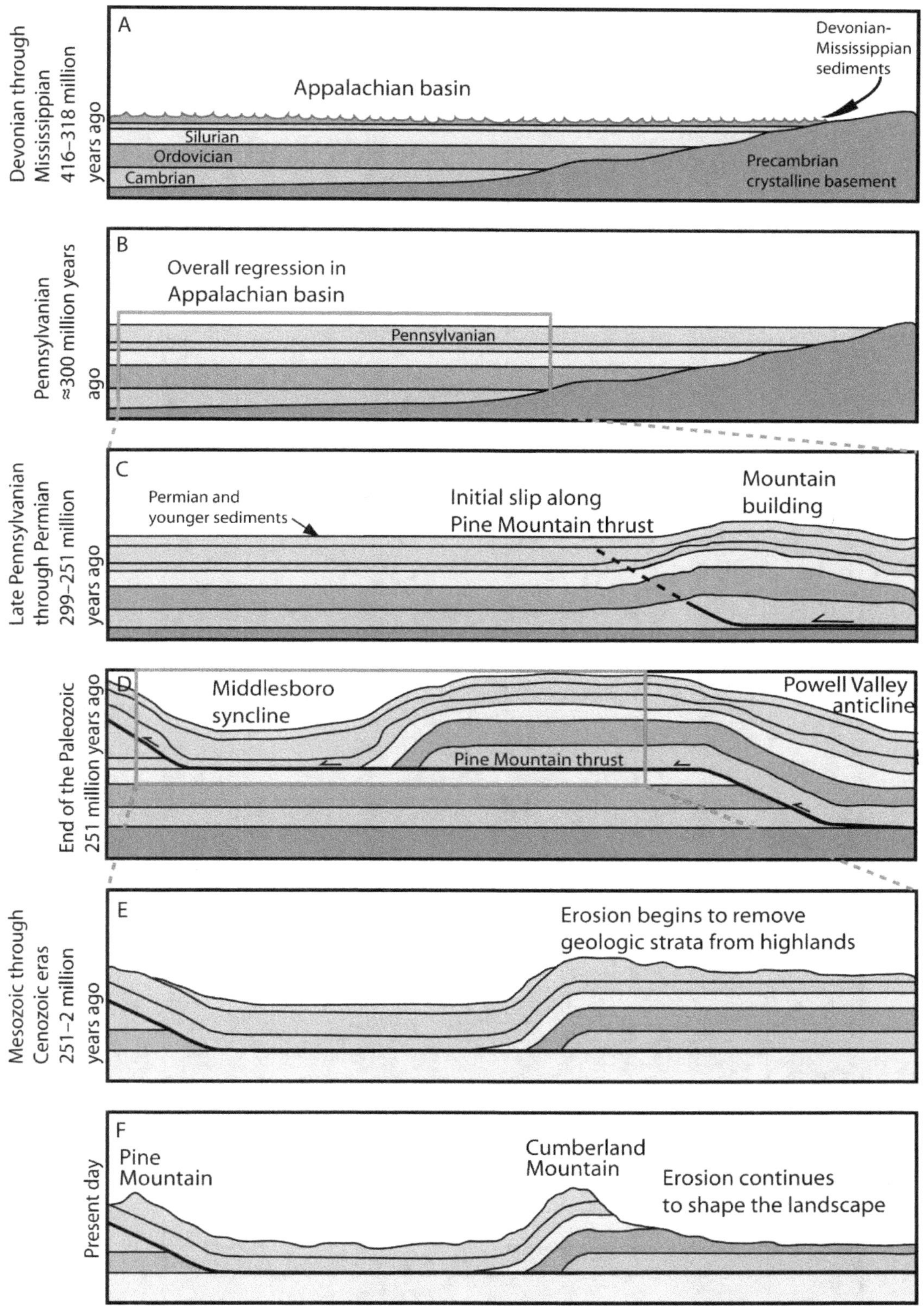

Figure 25. Landscape evolution. This generalized diagram shows the evolution of the landscape at Cumberland Gap National Historical Park. Note, drawings are not to scale and some structural elements such as the Doublings fault zone are omitted for graphical clarity. Graphic by Trista L. Thornberry-Ehrlich (Colorado State University) from information in McFarlan (1958), Englund (1964), and Englund and Harris (1961).

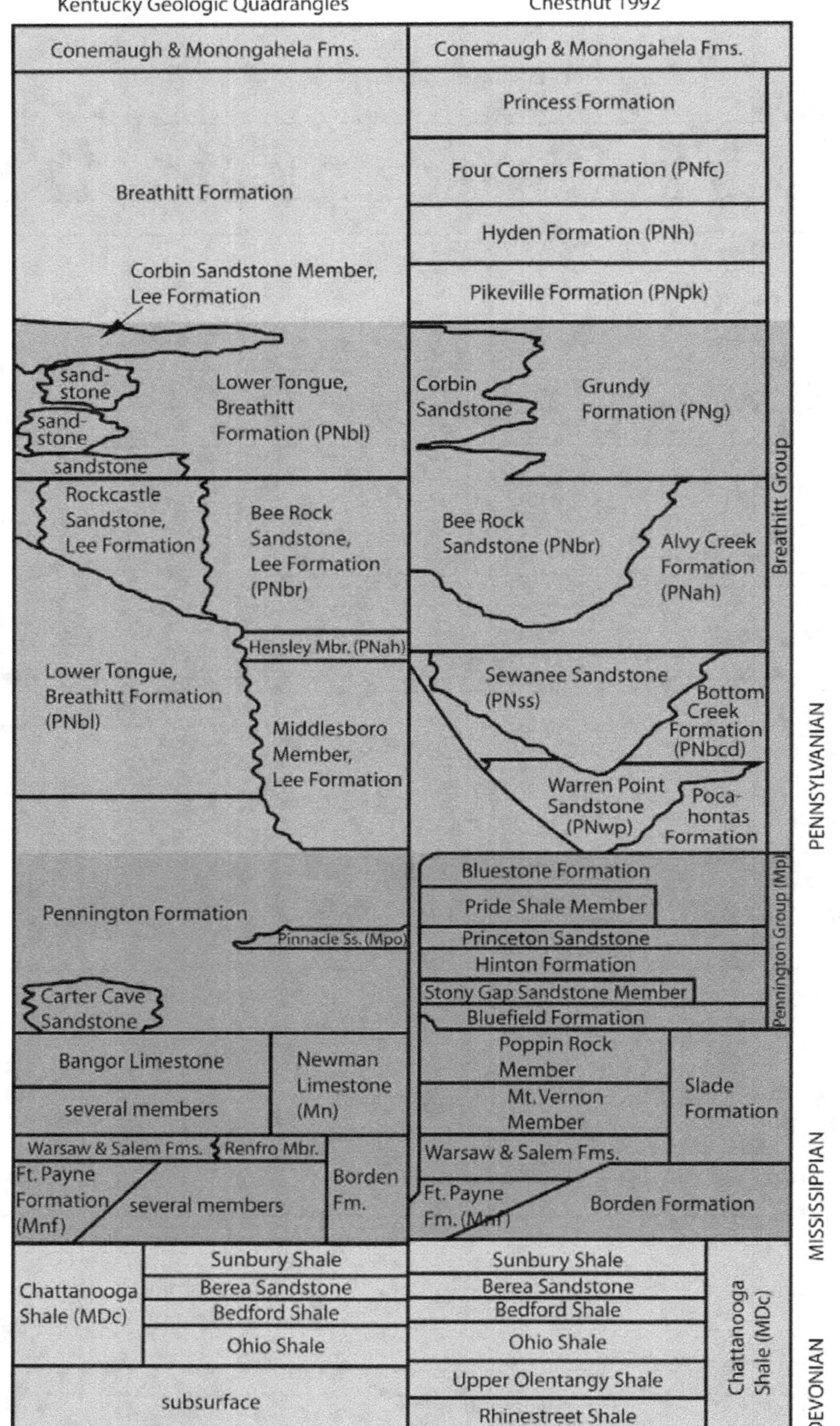

Figure 26. Stratigraphic columns. This correlative stratigraphic column shows the bedrock geologic units and nomenclature used in eastern Kentucky after Chestnut (1992). Older system on the left is after Englund et al. (1964), Englund (1964), and Rice (1978). The GRI digital geologic map units primarily follow the system of Chestnut (1992) with few exceptions. GRI map unit symbols are indicated in parentheses. Graphic is adapted from figure 4 in Milam et al. (2005) by Trista L. Thornberry-Ehrlich (Colorado State University).

Geologic Map Data

This section summarizes the geologic map data available for Cumberland Gap National Historical Park. It includes a fold-out geologic map overview and a summary table that lists each map unit displayed on the digital geologic map for the park. Complete GIS data are included on the accompanying CD and are also available at the Geologic Resources Inventory (GRI) publications website: http://www.nature.nps.gov/geology/inventory/gre_publications.cfm.

Geologic Maps

Geologic maps facilitate an understanding of an area's geologic framework and the evolution of its present landscape. Using designated colors and symbols, geologic maps portray the spatial distribution and relationships of rocks and unconsolidated deposits. Geologic maps also may show geomorphic features, structural interpretations, and locations of past geologic hazards that may be prone to future activity. Additionally, anthropogenic features such as mines and quarries may be indicated on geologic maps.

Source Maps

The Geologic Resources Inventory (GRI) team converts digital and/or paper source maps into the GIS formats that conform to the GRI GIS data model. The GRI digital geologic map product also includes essential elements of the source maps including unit descriptions, map legend, map notes, references, and figures. The GRI team used the following source maps to create the digital geologic data for Cumberland Gap National Historical Park:

Digital Sources

Mullins, J. E. 2003. Spatial database of the Ewing quadrangle, Kentucky-Virginia (scale 1:24,000). Digitally Vectorized Geological Quadrangle DVGQ-12_172. Kentucky Geological Survey, Lexington, Kentucky, USA.

Conley, T. J. 2003. Spatial database of the Kayjay quadrangle and part of the Fork Ridge quadrangle, Bell and Knox Counties, Kentucky (scale 1:24,000). Digitally Vectorized Geological Quadrangle DVGQ-12_1505. Kentucky Geological Survey, Lexington, Kentucky, USA.

Sparks, T. N. and J. R. Lambert. 2003. Spatial database of the Middlesboro North quadrangle, Kentucky (scale 1:24,000). Digitally Vectorized Geological Quadrangle DVGQ-12_1663. Kentucky Geological Survey, Lexington, Kentucky, USA.

Thompson, M. F. 2003. Spatial database of the Middlesboro South quadrangle, Tennessee-Kentucky-Virginia (scale 1:24,000). Digitally Vectorized Geological Quadrangle DVGQ-12_301. Kentucky Geological Survey, Lexington, Kentucky, USA.

Crawford, M. M. 2003. Spatial database of the Rose Hill quadrangle, Harlan County, Kentucky (scale 1:24,000). Digitally Vectorized Geological Quadrangle DVGQ-12_1121. Kentucky Geological Survey, Lexington, Kentucky, USA.

Johnson, T. L. 2003. Spatial database of the Varilla quadrangle, Kentucky-Virginia (scale 1:24,000). Digitally Vectorized Geological Quadrangle DVGQ-12_190. Kentucky Geological Survey, Lexington, Kentucky, USA.

Energy and Minerals Section, Kentucky Geological Survey, University of Kentucky, 10-May-2005, kyog83v10: Kentucky Oil and Gas Well Data, NAD 83 Version 10. Kentucky Geological Survey, Lexington, Kentucky, USA.

Paper Sources

Brent, W. B. 1988. Geologic Map and Mineral Resources Summary of the Back Valley Quadrangle, Tennessee (scale 1:24,000). GQ-161 SE. Tennessee Division of Geology, Nashville, Tennessee, USA.

Harris, L. D., J. G. Stephens, and R. L. Miller. 1962. Geology of the Coleman Gap quadrangle, Tennessee and Virginia (scale 1:24,000). GQ-188. U.S. Geological Survey, Reston, Virginia, USA.

Englund, K. J., H. L. Smith, L. D. Harris, and J. G. Stephens. 1963. Geology of the Ewing quadrangle, Kentucky and Virginia (scale 1:24,000). Map 1142-B. U.S. Geological Survey, Reston, Virginia, USA.

Kohl, M. S. and C. R.Sykes. 1991. Geologic Map and Mineral Resources Summary of the Fork Ridge Quadrangle, Tennessee. (scale 1:24,000). GQ-144 SE. Tennessee Division of Geology, Nashville, Tennessee, USA.

Rice, C. L. and E. K. Maughan. 1978. Geologic map of the Kayjay quadrangle and part of the Fork Ridge quadrangle, Bell and Knox Counties, Kentucky (scale 1:24,000). GQ-1505. U.S. Geological Survey, Reston, Virginia, USA.

Englund, K. J., J. B. Roen, and A. O. Delaney. 1964. Geology of the Middlesboro North quadrangle, Kentucky (scale 1:24,000). GQ-300. U.S. Geological Survey, Reston, Virginia, USA.

Englund, K. J. 1964. Geology of the Middlesboro South quadrangle, Tennessee-Kentucky-Virginia (scale 1:24,000). GQ-301. U.S. Geological Survey, Reston, Virginia, USA.

Maughan, E. K. and J. F. Tazelaar. 1973. Geologic map of part of the Rose Hill quadrangle, Harlan County, Kentucky (scale 1:24,000). GQ-1121. U.S. Geological Survey, Reston, Virginia, USA.

Englund, K. J., E. R. Landis, and H. L. Smith. 1963. Geology of the Varilla quadrangle, Kentucky-Virginia (scale 1:24,000). GQ-190. U.S. Geological Survey, Reston, Virginia, USA.

Harris, L. D. 1965. Geologic map of the Wheeler quadrangle, Claiborne County, Tennessee and Lee County, Virginia (scale 1:24,000). GQ-435. U.S. Geological Survey, Reston, Virginia, USA.

These source maps provided information for the "Geologic Issues," "Geologic Features and Processes," and "Geologic History" sections of this report.

Geologic GIS Data

The GRI team implements a GIS data model that standardizes map deliverables. The data model is included on the enclosed CD and is also available online (http://science.nature.nps.gov/im/inventory/geology/GeologyGISDataModel.cfm). This data model dictates GIS data structure including layer architecture, feature attribution, and relationships within ESRI ArcGIS software. The GRI team digitized the data for Cumberland Gap National Historical Park using data model version 2.1.

GRI digital geologic data for Cumberland Gap National Historical Park are included on the attached CD and are available through the NPS Natural Resource Information Portal (https://nrinfo.nps.gov/ Reference.mvc/Search). Enter "GRI" as the search text and select Cumberland Gap National Historical Park from the unit list. The following components and geology data layers are part of the data set:

- Data in ESRI geodatabase and shapefile GIS formats
- Layer files with feature symbology (see list below)
- Federal Geographic Data Committee (FGDC)–compliant metadata
- A help file (.hlp) document that contains all of the ancillary map information and graphics, including geologic unit correlation tables and map unit descriptions, legends, and other information captured from source maps.
- An ESRI map document file (.mxd) that displays the digital geologic data

Geology data layers in the Cumberland Gap National Historical Park GIS data.

Data Layer	Code	On Geologic Map Overview?
Geologic Point Features (Coal Outcrops)	GPF	No
Geologic Attitude and Observation Points	ATD	No
Map Symbology	SYM	Yes
Mine Point Features	MIN	No
Geologic Cross Section Lines	SEC	No
Structure Contours, Base Fire Clay Coal Bed	CN1	No
Structure Contours, Base Manchester Coal Bed	CN2	No
Structure Contours, Base Upper Elkhorn No. 2 (Jellico) Coal Bed	CN3	No
Structure Contours, Top Upper Elkhorn No. 2 (Jellico) Coal Bed	CN4	No
Faults	FLT	Yes
Folds	FLD	Yes
Linear Geologic Units	GLN	No
Mine Feature Lines	MFL	No
Mine Area Features	MAF	No
Mine Area Feature Boundaries	MAFA	No
Surficial Contacts	SURA	Yes
Geologic Contacts	GLGA	Yes
Surficial Units	SUR	Yes
Geologic Units	GLG	Yes

Note: All data layers may not be visible on the geologic map overview graphic.

Geologic Map Overview

The fold-out geologic map overview displays the GRI digital geologic data draped over a shaded relief image of Cumberland Gap National Historical Park and includes basic geographic information. For graphic clarity and legibility, not all GIS feature classes are visible on the overview. The digital elevation data and geographic information are not included with the GRI digital geologic GIS data for the park, but are available online from a variety of sources.

Map Unit Properties Table

The geologic units listed in the fold-out map unit properties table correspond to the accompanying digital geologic data. Following overall structure of the report, the table highlights the geologic issues, features, and processes associated with each map unit. The units, their relationships, and the series of events the created them are highlighted in the "Geologic History" section. Please refer to the geologic timescale (fig. 20) for the geologic period and age associated with each unit.

Use Constraints

Graphic and written information provided in this section is not a substitute for site-specific investigations, and ground-disturbing activities should neither be permitted nor denied based upon the information provided here. Minor inaccuracies may exist regarding the location of geologic features relative to other geologic or geographic features on the overview graphic. Based on the source map scale (1:24,000) and U.S. National Map Accuracy Standards, geologic features represented here are within 12 meters / 40 feet (horizontally) of their true location.

Please contact GRI with any questions.

Cumberland Gap National Historical Park
Kentucky, Tennessee, Virginia

National Park Service
U.S. Department of the Interior

Overview of Digital Geologic Data for Cumberland Gap NHP

These figures were prepared as part of the NPS Geologic Resources Division's Geologic Resources Inventory. They are an overview of compiled digital geologic data, and not a substitute for site-specific investigations.

Minor inaccuracies may exist regarding the location of geologic features relative to other geologic or geographic features on the figure. Based on the source map scales (1:24,000) and U.S. National Map Accuracy Standards, geologic features represented here are within 12 meters / 40 feet of their true location.

The source maps used in creation of the digital geologic data product include publications from the Kentucky Geological Survey, Tennessee Division of Geology, and U.S. Geological Survey (see Geologic Map Data Section in report for specific sources).

Digital geologic data and cross sections for Cumberland Gap National Historical Park, and all other digital geologic data prepared as part of the Geologic Resources Inventory, are available online at the NPS Natural Resource Information Portal: https://nrinfo.nps.gov/Reference.mvc/Search. (Enter "GRI" as the search text and select Cumberland Gap National Historical Park from the unit list.)

Produced by the Geologic Resources Inventory

September 2011

Cumberland Gap National Historical Park
Kentucky, Tennessee, Virginia

National Park Service
U.S. Department of the Interior

Overview of Digital Geologic Data for Cumberland Gap NHP

SHEET 2: WESTERN EXTENT

Cumberland Gap
Pinnacle Overlook
Gap (Cudjo) Cave
Visitor Center
Fern Lake
25E
58

North

0 1 2 3 4 5 6 Kilometers
0 1 2 3 Miles

Produced by the Geologic Resources Inventory

September 2011

Overview of Digital Geologic Data for Cumberland Gap NHP

SHEET 3: EASTERN EXTENT

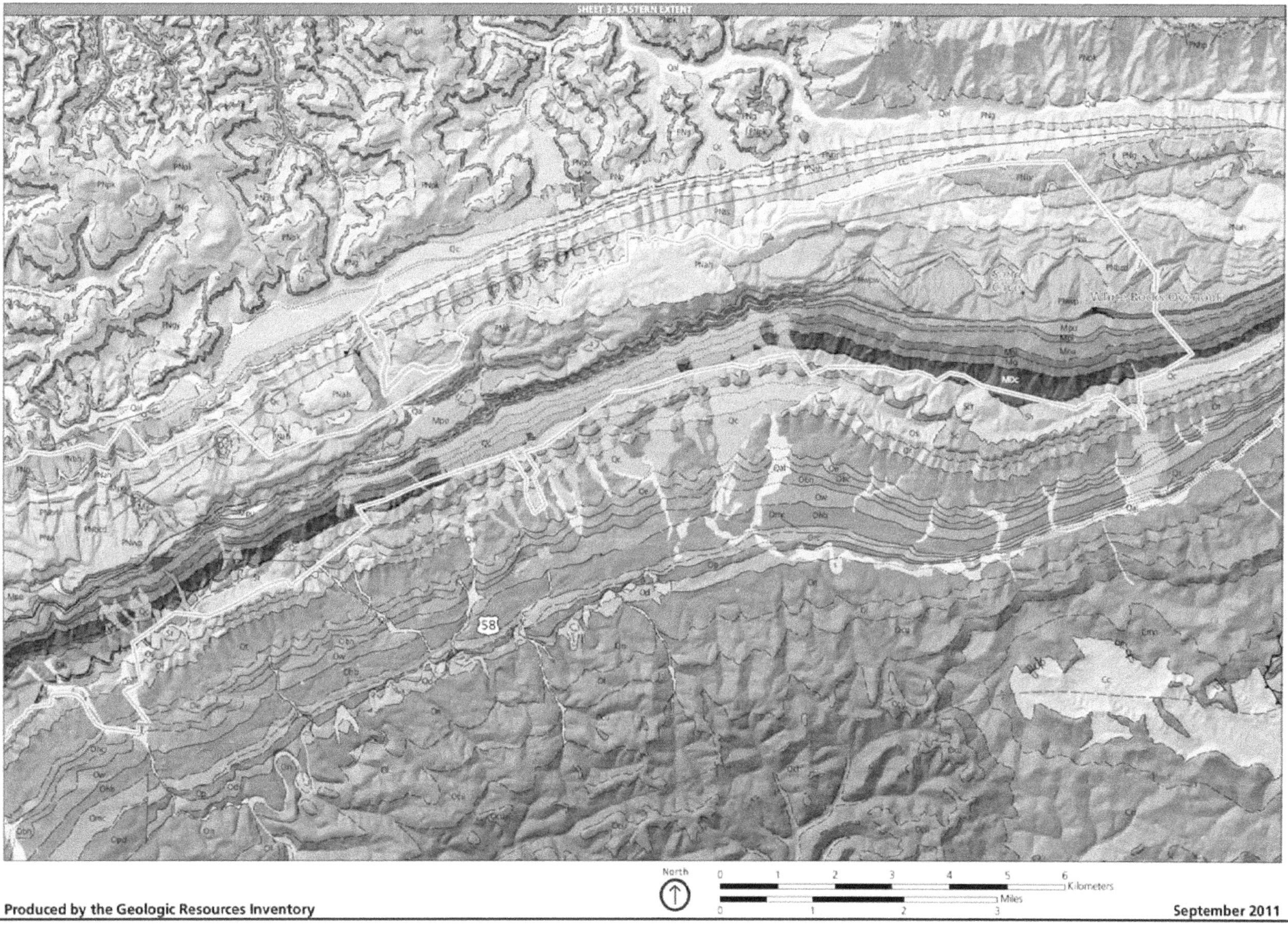
58
White Rocks Overlook
North
0 1 2 3 4 5 6 Kilometers
0 1 2 3 Miles

Produced by the Geologic Resources Inventory

September 2011

Map Unit Properties Table: Cumberland Gap National Historical Park

Gray-shaded rows indicate units included within the GIS data for Cumberland Gap National Historical Park but not mapped within the park.

Age	Group Name	Map Unit (Symbol)	Geologic Description	Geologic Issues	Geologic Features and Processes	Geologic History and Park Connections
QUATERNARY		Artificial fill (*Qf*) Alluvium (***Qal***) Alluvial fan deposits (***Qaf***) Terrace deposits (***Qt***)	***Qf*** consists of stable fill on gentle slopes and stabilized engineered structures. ***Qal*** includes sand, silt, clay, and gravel in well-sorted, thin-bedded laminations. Unit is relatively rich in organic matter. ***Qaf*** contains boulders, gravel, sand, and silt in poorly sorted deposits intermingling with colluvium locally. ***Qt*** consists of boulders, gravel, sand, silt, and clay 1.5–6 m (5–20 ft) above the river level. ***Qf*** and ***Qal*** mapped within the park.	***Qaf*** underlies active streambanks and should be avoided for most development. ***Qaf*** is associated with active ravines and areas prone to mass wasting. Very low erosion resistance.	May contain historic and prehistoric remains. Modern remains and fossils present in float Sand, gravel, silt, clay ***Qal*** underlies riparian habitat along the edges of streams and rivers.	***Qal*** contains gravel, pebbles, cobbles, and occasional boulders of quartz, chert, sandstone, siltstone, limestone, and coal from Mississippian and Pennsylvanian provenance from the surrounding highlands.
QUATERNARY		Landslide deposits (***Qls***) Colluvium (***Qc***)	***Qls*** contains large slumped sandstone blocks in poorly sorted to unsorted piles. ***Qc*** contains angular to rounded pebbles, cobbles, and boulders in finer grained matrices of sand, silt, and clay. Units commonly show hummocky topography and may reach thicknesses greater than 24 m (80 ft). ***Qc*** mapped within the park.	Units are associated with active mass wasting and slope processes and should be avoided for most development. Prone to slumping, sliding, and blockfall. Active scarps are often present associated with these units. Very low to low erosion resistance.	May contain historic and prehistoric remains. Modern remains and fossils present in float Sand, silt, clay, boulders, angular blocks May provide burrow habitat.	Units record active processes of weathering and erosion, diminishing the highlands and filling low-lying areas with mixed sediment.
QUATERNARY		Terrace deposits: high level terrace deposits (***Qth***) low level terrace deposits (***Qtl***)	***Qth*** consists of boulders, sand, silt, and clay in high-level deposits above active waterways. ***Qtl*** contains boulders, sand, silt, and clay in unconsolidated deposits from local sources.	Units may be prone to slumping and mass wasting when perched above active areas of erosion. May become undercut and unstable on slopes. Very low erosion resistance	May contain historic and prehistoric remains. Modern remains and fossils present in float Sand, silt, clay, boulders Units may be perched aquifers and provide well-drained substrates.	Units record the evolution of the modern drainage systems draining both sides of the mountains within the park area.
MIDDLE PENNSYLVANIAN	Breathitt Group	Breathitt Group, intensely deformed: (***PNbd***) Unnamed coal bed in (***PNbdc2***) Unnamed sandstone member (***PNbdss***) Unnamed coal bed at base of unnamed sandstone member (***PNbdc1***)	Units contain various units of the Breathitt Group including shale, siltstone, sandstone, and coal that have been macrobrecciated and shattered in fault blocks within Middlesboro Basin. Deformation is ascribed to meteorite impact.	Units are prone to erosion and may fail when exposed on slopes and/or undercut. Potential for mass wasting. Low erosion resistance.	City of Middlesboro sits within the ancient meteorite impact structure. Fossils, if present, may be too deformed to identify Shale, siltstone, sandstone, coal, limestone (all deformed) Thin coal beds and shales may weather to produce soils containing high iron and manganese contents.	Units record the tremendous energy involved with a meteorite impact including faulting, brecciation, and slumping. Units record the Middlesboro meteorite impact and is present in numerous outcrops surrounding the town within the park area. Rocks exposed today were beneath the actual crater. The crater has long-since eroded away.

Gray-shaded rows indicate units included within the GIS data for Cumberland Gap National Historical Park but not mapped within the park.

Age	Group Name	Map Unit (Symbol)	Geologic Description	Geologic Issues	Geologic Features and Processes	Geologic History and Park Connections
MIDDLE PENNSYLVANIAN	Breathitt Group	Four Corners Formation: (*PNfc*) Reynolds Sandstone Member (*PNfcre*) Hazard coal bed (*PNfchz*) Unnamed coal bed between Hazard and Haddix coal beds (*PNfcc1*) Haddix coal bed (*PNfchd*) Magoffin Member (*PNfcmag*)	***PNfc*** consists of sandstone, siltstone, shale, coal, and limestone. contains a basal portion, ***PNfcmag***, of dark gray, silty, calcareous, fossiliferous shale and dark gray to black, micaceous silty, nodular limestone grading upward into interbedded siltstone and shale. Unit also contains abundant coal beds ***PNfchz***, ***PNfcc1***, and ***PNfchd***. ***PNfcre*** contains fine-grained, thick-bedded to massive, light-gray sandstone and medium-gray shale.	Heterogeneous nature of units may render them unstable on slopes and prone to sliding and blockfall. ***PNfcmag*** may be thick and prone to weathering and erosion. Blocks of sandstone may spall off ledges. Moderate to low (shales) erosion resistance.	Units contain named coal horizons that may have been mining targets. Marine fossils in ***PNfcmag***. Sparse plant fossils in shales and sandstones above coal beds. *Stigmaria* in clays beneath coal beds. Sandstone, siltstone, shale, coal, limestone. Coals include Hazard No. 7 (High Splint), Hazard zone (Red Springs and Morris), and Haddix zone (Low Splint of Hignite Formation). Thin coal beds and shales may weather to produce soils containing high iron and manganese contents.	Units record shifting depositional environments and vast swamps present during this time in geologic history. Distinctive coal beds provide important marker horizons throughout the region.
		Upper part of Breathitt Group, undifferentiated (*PNbu*) Hyden Formation (*PNh*) Jesse Sandstone Member, Hyden Formation (*PNhj*) Unnamed coal between Magoffin Member and Fire Clay rider coal bed (*PNbuc4*) Unnamed coal bed between Haddix and Fire Clay coal beds (*PNhc1*) Fire Clay rider coal bed (*PNhfr*) Fire Clay coal bed (*PNhfc*)	***PNbu*** consists of silty, gray, laminated, micaceous shale that weathers to a brown color. Unit also contains dark to light gray, massive to bedded siltstone that weathers yellowish-brown. Fine- to coarse-grained, thin-bedded to massive, light gray sandstone also presnt in beds up to 12 m (40 ft) thick. In upper reaches of the unit, sandstone can be up to 30 m (100 ft) thick. Sandstones are discontinuous laterally. PNbuc4, ***PNbuc3***, ***PNbuc2***, and ***PNbuc1*** are unnamed coal seams within the ***PNbu***. ***PNh*** contains sandstone, siltstone, shale, coal, and minor limestone. The base of the unit shifts from the Kendrick Shale Member to the Poplar Lick (Amburgy) coal zone. ***PNh*** contains the ***PNhc1***, ***PNhfr***, ***PNhfc***, ***PNhw*** (see below), ***PNham*** (see below), and ***PNhams*** (see below) coal beds. ***PNhj*** is a fine- to coarse-grained, massive, cross-bedded sandstone that contains conglomeratic beds at its base with white quartz pebbles, clay pellets, and lithic clasts. ***PNbu***, ***PNh***, **and** ***PNhfr*** mapped within the park.	***PNhj*** is associated with cliff formation and thus may be prone to block fall and landslides. Clays beneath coal beds and coals may influence water movement and slope stability. Moderate to high erosion resistance for cliff-forming sandstones, low for shales.	Units contain named coal horizons that may have been mining targets. ***PNbu*** contains macerated plant remains, fossil leaves, stem imprints, *Stigmaria*, brachiopods, gastropods, cephalopods, and osctracods at the base of the unit. Shale, sandstone, siltstone, coal, underclay, siderite nodules, conglomerate with quartz pebbles between 0.64 and 1.3 cm (0.25 and 0.5 in.) in diameter. Thin coal beds and shales may weather to produce soils containing high iron and manganese contents.	Units record shifting sea level and depositional environments from coastal-deltaic to open marine. Coals represent vast mires (swamps). Distinctive coal beds provide important marker horizons throughout the region. Some marine shales are also distinctive marker horizons.
		Puckett Sandstone Member, Hyden Formation (*PNhp*) Whitesburg coal bed (*PNhw*) Amburgy coal bed (*PNham*) Amburgy coal bed, Sterling coal bed part (*PNhams*) Unnamed coal seams between Poplar Lick and Darby coal beds (*PNbuc3*)	***PNhp*** is a fine- to coarse-grained, massive, cross-bedded, micaceous, light gray sandstone. Some medium gray shale, stilstone, coal, and underclay interbeds present locally. ***PNham*** and ***PNhams*** mapped within the park.	***PNhp*** is associated with cliff formation and thus may be prone to block fall and landslides. Calcareous shales may be prone to dissolution and could undermine more resistant rock layers above. Clays beneath coal beds and coals may influence water movement and slope stability. Moderate to high erosion resistance for cliff-forming sandstones, low for shales.	Units contain named coal horizons that may have been mining targets. Sparse marine fossils in shales. Sparse plant fossils in shales and sandstones above coal beds. *Stigmaria* in clays beneath coal beds. Sandstone, shale, stilstone, coal, underclay, ellipsoidal limestone concretions, and siderite nodules. Cliffs provide raptor habitat and support upland species.	Units record shifting sea level and depositional environments from coastal-deltaic to open marine. Coals represent vast mires (swamps). Distinctive coal beds provide important marker horizons throughout the region. Some marine shales are also distinctive marker horizons.

Gray-shaded rows indicate units included within the GIS data for Cumberland Gap National Historical Park but not mapped within the park.

Age	Group Name	Map Unit (Symbol)	Geologic Description	Geologic Issues	Geologic Features and Processes	Geologic History and Park Connections
MIDDLE PENNSYLVANIAN	Breathitt Group	Mingo Formation (*PNm*) Pikeville Formation (*PNpk*)	***Pnm*** contains medium gray to black shale interbedded with silty shale, siltstone, and fine-grained, light gray, micacesou, thin- to thick-bedded, crossbedded sandstone. Unit also contains coal and underclay. ***PNpk*** contains siltstone, shale, sandstone, and coal. The sandstones are fine- to medium-grained, massive, and crossbedded. Coal beds within ***PNpk*** include ***PNpkd*** (see below), ***PNpkc3*** (see below), ***PNpke3*** (see below), ***PNpke2*** (see below), ***PNpkc2*** (see below), ***PNpke1*** (see below), ***PNpkc1*** (see below), and ***PNpklbg*** (see below).	Heterogeneous nature of units may render them unstable on slopes and prone to sliding and blockfall. Sandstones within ***PNpk*** are associated with cliff formation and thus may be prone to block fall and landslides. Clays beneath coal beds and coals may influence water movement and slope stability. Moderate to high erosion resistance for cliff-forming sandstones, low for shales.	Units contain named coal horizons that may have been mining targets. Fossil leaf and stem imprints, *Stigmaria* in clays beneath coal beds Shale, siltstone, sandstone, coal, underclays, limestone concretions, and siderite nodules. Cliffs provide raptor habitat and support upland species.	Units record shifting sea level and depositional environments from coastal-deltaic to open marine. Coals represent vast mires (swamps). Distinctive coal beds provide important marker horizons throughout the region. Some marine shales are also distinctive marker horizons.
		Middle part of Breathitt Group, undifferentiated (*PNbm*) Darby (Upper Elkhorn No. 3.5) coal bed (*PNpkd*) Unnamed coal seam between Darby and Upper Elkhorn No. 2 (Jellico) coal beds in upper Breathitt Group (*PNbuc2*) Unnamed coal bed between Darby and Upper Elkhorn No. 2 (Jellico) coal beds in Pikeville Formation (*PNpkc3*) Upper Elkhorn No. 3 coal (*PNpke3*) Upper Elkhorn No. 2 (Jellico) coal bed (*PNpke2*)	***PNbm*** consists of shale, siltstone, sandstone, and coal. The shale is light to dark gray, micaceous, carbonaceous, calcareous, and interbedded with thin layers of sandstone. Sandstone is fine- to medium-grained, poorly to well sorted, thin- to thick-bedded, micaceous with some quartzose and carbonaceous lenses locally. Some beds are up to 15 m (50 ft) thick. Deformed coal layers may be up to 0.5 m (1.5 ft) thick near the top of the unit. ***PNpkd*** and ***PNpke2*** mapped within the park.	Units are intensely sheared locally which may render them susceptible to increased erosion and mass wasting. Heterogeneous nature of units may render them unstable when exposed on slopes. Calcareous shales may be prone to dissolution. ***PNbm*** is associated with alluvium and colluvium deposits and thus may crop out in a setting prone to slope processes. Clays beneath coal beds and coals may influence water movement and slope stability. Moderate to high erosion resistance for cliff-forming sandstones, low for shales.	Units contain named coal horizons that may have been mining targets. Sparse marine fossils in shales. Sparse plant fossils in shales and sandstones above coal beds. *Stigmaria* in clays beneath coal beds. Shale, siltstone, sandstone, coal, underclays, limestone concretions, and siderite nodules. Thin coal beds and shales may weather to produce soils containing high iron and manganese contents.	Where this unit is within the Middlesboro Basin, ***PNbm*** records pervasive brittle deformation manifested as sheared zones and slickensides possibly caused by the Middlesboro meteorite impact event. Its original depositional environment was much like the above units, but was then later deformed during the impact.
		Hance Formation (*PNha*) Unnamed coal bed between Upper Elkhorn No. 2 (Jellico) and Lower Elkhorn (Blue Gem) coal beds (*PNpkc2*) Lower Elkhorn (Blue Gem) coal bed (*PNpke1*) Unnamed coal bed between Lower Elkhorn (Blue Gem) and Manchester coal beds (*PNpkc1*) Little Blue Gem coal bed (*PNpklbg*)	***PNha*** contains medium to dark gray shale and silty shale interbedded with siltstone, coal, underclay, or fine-grained sandstone. Sandstone tends to be light gray, fine- to medium-grained, micaceous, and thin- to thick-bedded. Sandstone weathers to buff or brown color and beds may reach 12 m (40 ft) thickness. ***PNha*** and ***PNpke1*** mapped within the park.	Shale rich unit may weather to clay and be prone to mass wasting processes of slumping and sliding where exposed on slopes. Heterogeneous nature of units may render them unstable on slopes and prone to sliding and blockfall. Clays beneath coal beds and coals may influence water movement and slope stability. Moderate to high erosion resistance for cliff-forming sandstones, low for shales.	Units contain named coal horizons that may have been mining targets. Fossil leaf and stem imprints, *Stigmaria* in clays beneath coal beds. Shale, siltstone, sandstone, underclay, coal, siderite nodules. Thin coal beds and shales may weather to produce soils containing high iron and manganese contents.	Units record shifting sea level and depositional environments from coastal-deltaic to open marine. Coals represent vast mires (swamps). Distinctive coal beds provide important marker horizons throughout the region. Some marine shales are also distinctive marker horizons.

Gray-shaded rows indicate units included within the GIS data for Cumberland Gap National Historical Park but not mapped within the park.

Age	Group Name	Map Unit (Symbol)	Geologic Description	Geologic Issues	Geologic Features and Processes	Geologic History and Park Connections
LOWER PENNSYLVANIAN	Breathitt Group	Manchester coal bed (*PNmn*) Grundy Formation (*PNg*) Unnamed sandstone member Grundy Formation (*PNgss*) Mason rider coal bed (*PNgmr*) Mason coal bed (*PNgma*) Unnamed coal beds in lower part of upper Breathitt Group (*PNbuc1*) Unnamed coal bed in Grundy Formation (*PNgc1*)	***PNg*** contains ***PNgy*** and ***PNgss*** as very fine- to medium-grained, micaceous sandstones. ***PNg*** also has the coal bed units of ***PNmn***, ***PNgmr***, ***PNgma***, ***PNgc1***, ***PNggh*** (see below), and ***PNgcf*** (see below). ***PNmn***, ***PNg***, ***PNgss***, ***PNgmr*** and ***PNgma*** mapped within the park.	***PNg*** contains cliff-forming sandstones, which may be prone to blockfall and sliding. Clays beneath coal beds and coals may influence water movement and slope stability. Moderate to high erosion resistance for cliff-forming sandstones, low for shales.	Units contain named coal horizons that may have been mining targets. Sparse marine fossils in shales (though fewer than in overlying units). Sparse plant fossils in shales and sandstones above coal beds. *Stigmaria* in clays beneath coal beds. Sandstone, shale, siltstone, coal, underclays, limestone concretions, and siderite nodules. Cliffs provide raptor habitat and support upland species.	Units record mixed, nearshore to swampy depositional environments during the Lower Pennsylvanian. Regional coals including the Lily (Manchester), Mason rider, Mason (Chenoa), Gray Hawk (Split Seam), Clear Fork, and Naese. These coal beds form prominent and correlative marker horizons across the region.
		Gray Hawk coal bed (*PNggh*) Lower part of Breathitt Group (*PNbl*) Clear Fork coal bed (*PNgcf*) Yellow Creek Sandstone Member, Grundy Formation (*PNgy*)	***PNbl*** contains fine- to coarse-grained, poorly to moderately sorted, thin- to thick-bedded, and white to dark gray sandstone, dark gray siltstone, and shale. Sandstone is locally friable, micaceous, crossbedded, and conglomeratic. ***PNgy*** includes very fine- to fine-grained, micaceous, light gray sandstone, and medium to dark gray shale. ***PNgcf*** and ***PNgy*** mapped within the park.	***PNbl***, in the Middlesboro basin, is associated with pervasive deformation structures. Deformation includes shear zones, fractures, and slickensides. Vertically dipping beds within the sandstone form prominent cliffs, which may be prone to blockfall and sliding. Locally friable sandstones may be unstable on slopes. ***PNgy*** contains cliff-forming sandstones, which may be prone to blockfall and sliding. Clays beneath coal beds and coals may influence water movement and slope stability. Moderate to high erosion resistance for cliff-forming sandstones, low for shales.	Units contain named coal horizons that may have been mining targets. Sparse marine fossils in shales (though fewer than in overlying units). Sparse plant fossils in shales and sandstones above coal beds. *Stigmaria* in clays beneath coal beds. Sandstone, siltstone, shale, ironstone concretions, conglomerate with quartz pebbles up to 2.5 cm (1 in.) in diameter, siderite nodules. Cliffs provide raptor habitat and support upland species.	***PNbl*** was formerly mapped as the Lee Formation, and is exposed in fault slices adjacent to Pine Mountain, and in the central uplift core of the Middlesboro Basin. Deformation within ***PNbl*** may be due in part to the Middlesboro meteorite impact event. Base of ***PNbl*** forms the sole of the Pine Mountain overthrust fault.
		Bee Rock Sandstone: (*PNbr*) Naese coal bed (*PNbrn*) Naese Sandstone Member, Upper part of Bee Rock Sandstone (*PNbru*) Unnamed coal bed in Naese Sandstone Member below Naese coal bed (*PNbrc1*) Lower part of Bee Rock Sandstone (*PNbrl*)	***PNbr*** consists of fine- to carose-grained, well sorted, locally silty, massive, and white to light gray sandstone, conglomeratic sandstone, siltstone, shale, and minor coal beds. Silstone and shale are micaceous, carbonaceous and medium to dark gray in outcrop. ***PNbr*** contains the Naese coal bed (***PNbrn***) as well as thin, unmapped coal layers. ***PNbru*** is the upper sandstone member within ***PNbr*** and contains ***PNbrc1***. ***PNbrl*** is the lower portion of ***PNbr***. ***PNbrc1*** is not mapped within the park.	***PNbr*** contains cliff-forming sandstones, which may be prone to blockfall and sliding especially where underlain by weaker, more friable shales. Clays beneath coal beds and coals may influence water movement and slope stability. Moderate to high erosion resistance for cliff-forming sandstones, low for shales.	Units contain named coal horizons that may have been mining targets. Sparse plant fossils in shales and sandstones above coal beds. *Stigmaria* in clays beneath coal beds. Coal layers may contain plant fossils. At the base of some sandstones within ***PNbr*** may contain lags of fossil logs and plant debris. Sandstone, conglomerate with quartz pebbles 0.5 to 5 cm (0.25 to 2 in.) in diameter, siltstone, shale, coal. Cliffs provide raptor habitat and support upland species.	***PNbr*** was originally part of the Lee Formation. ***PNbr*** forms cliffs and hogbacks along the south slope of Pine Mountain with shales forming slope breaks or swales between sandstone cliffs. Sandstones formed in vast south to southwest flowing rivers. Some of which were converted to estuaries during rising sea level.

Gray-shaded rows indicate units included within the GIS data for Cumberland Gap National Historical Park but not mapped within the park.

Age	Group Name	Map Unit (Symbol)	Geologic Description	Geologic Issues	Geologic Features and Processes	Geologic History and Park Connections
LOWER PENNSYLVANIAN	Breathitt Group	Hance Formation (*PNha*) Unnamed coal bed between Upper Elkhorn No. 2 (Jellico) and Lower Elkhorn (Blue Gem) coal beds (*PNpkc2*) Lower Elkhorn (Blue Gem) coal bed (*PNpke1*) Unnamed coal bed between Lower Elkhorn (Blue Gem) and Manchester coal beds (*PNpkc1*) Little Blue Gem coal bed (*PNpklbg*)	***PNah*** contains sandy, carbonaceous, micaceous, thin-bedded, medium to dark gray shale and siltstone. Unit also includes very fine- to medium-grained, well to poorly sorted, thin- to thick-bedded micaceous and carbonaceous sandstone. The Tunnel coal bed crops out within ***PNah***. Unit also includes ***PNahst***. ***PNahus*** contains fine- to medium-grained, micaceous, light gray sandstone that weathers to brown; argillaceous to sandy, gray, laminated siltstone; and dark gray, carbonaceous shale. Some sandstones within ***PNahus*** are coarse-grained, non-conglomeratic, and form prominent outcrops.	***PNah*** contains cliff-forming sandstones, which may be prone to blockfall and sliding especially where underlain by weaker, more friable shales. Shales within ***PNahus*** may be friable and create zones of weakness in the rock column. Clays beneath coal beds and coals may influence water movement and slope stability. Moderate to moderately high erosion resistance for sandstone in ***PNah***; moderate to low for shales	Units contain named coal horizons that may have been mining targets. Sparse marine fossils in shales. Sparse plant fossils in shales and sandstones above coal beds. *Stigmaria* in clays beneath coal beds. Shale, siltstone, sandstone, coal, underclay, limestone concretions, siderite nodules. Cliffs provide raptor habitat and support upland species.	Shales and siltstones underlie swales below the sandstone ridges created by ***PNah***. Distinctive coal beds provide valuable marker horizons for regional mapping and correlation.
		Sewanee and Warren Point Sandstones (*PNsw*) Sewanee Sandstone (*PNss*) Lower part of Sewanee Sandstone (*PNlss*)	Unit ***PNsw*** consists of conglomeratic sandstone, sandstone, siltstone, and shale. Sandstone layers are white to light gray, fine- to coarse-grained, massive, distinctively crossbedded. Siltstone and shale are olive to dark gray, micaceous, carbonaceous, interbedded and/or grading into sandstone. ***PNss*** is conglomerate, sandstone, siltstone, and shale; locally divided into four distinct ledges. ***PNlss*** contains fine- to coarse-grained, massive, crossbedded, conglomeratic, white to light gray sandstone. ***PNss*** and ***PNlss*** mapped within the park.	Conglomeratic sandstone forms resistant ledges often separated by narrow valleys underlain by siltstone and shale. Ledges and cliffs may be sites of active slope processes such as block fall and sliding. Clays beneath coal beds and coals may influence water movement and slope stability. Moderate to high erosion resistance for conglomeratic sandstone.	Units form prominent cliffs that acted as orientation points for early migrations through the Cumberland Gap. No fossils documented in park; potential for fossil plants exist. Conglomeratic sandstone with pebbles up to 7.6 cm (3 in.) in diameter, sandstone, siltstone, shale. Ledges provide upland habitat forming bald hogbacks separated by valleys.	***PNss*** and ***PNlss*** form hogbacks on top of Rocky Face and on the northwest slope of Cumberland Mountain. Sandstones formed in vast south to southwest flowing rivers. Some of which were converted to estuaries during rising sea level.
		Dark Ridge Shale Member, Bottom Creek Formation and Warren Point Sandstone (*PNdcbw*) Dark Ridge Shale Member, Bottom Creek Formation (*PNbcd*) Cumberland Gap coal bed (*PNbcdcg*) White Rocks sandstone bed, Warren Point Sandstone (*PNwpw*) Warren Point Sandstone (*PNwp*)	***PNdcbw*** consists of dark gray to light olive-gray shale interbedded with fine- to coarse-grained, crossbedded, light gray to white sandstone. ***PNbcd*** contains medium to dark gray, calcareous shale and siltstone, greenish clay shale, ripple-laminated siltstone, and fine-grained sandstone. Unit also includes the Cumberland Gap coal bed, ***PNbcdcg***. ***PNwpw*** contains fine- to coarse-grained, massive, crossbedded, conglomeratic, white to very light gray sandstone. ***PNwp*** includes conglomerate, sandstone, and siltstone.	Sandstone forms prominent bluffs, which may be prone to blockfall if fractured and/or undercut by less resistant underlying units. Clays beneath coal beds and coals may influence water movement and slope stability. Potential impacts from climbers at White Rocks area could include degradation of rock face and trampling of vegetation (one endangered species is found near White Rocks cliffs). Moderate erosion resistance.	Units form prominent cliffs ("White Rocks") that acted as orientation points for early migrations through the Cumberland Gap. Sand Cave formed within ***PNwp***. Shales and coal layers may contain sparse plant fossils. Some plant fossils (logs) are possible at the base of some sandstones. Sandstone, shale, coal, underclay, conglomeratic sandstone with pebbles 1.3 to 1.5 cm (0.5 to 1 in.) in diameter. Cliffs provide raptor habitat and support upland species.	***PNbcd*** was previously mapped as a member of the Lee Formation. ***PNwp*** was originally mapped as White Rocks Sandstone Member or Chadwell Member of the Lee Formation. Sandstones formed in vast south to southwest flowing rivers. Some of which were converted to estuaries during rising sea level. ***PNcbd*** records a rise in sea level and restricted marine conditions.

Gray-shaded rows indicate units included within the GIS data for Cumberland Gap National Historical Park but not mapped within the park.

Age	Group Name	Map Unit (Symbol)	Geologic Description	Geologic Issues	Geologic Features and Processes	Geologic History and Park Connections
LOWER PENNSYLVANIAN-MISSISSIPPIAN	Breathitt and Pennington Groups	Lower part of Breathitt Group and Pennington Group (*PNMbp*)	Unit contains alternating zones of light olive-gray to light gray sandstone and greenish gray shale and siltstone. In lower portions of the unit, sandstone is thin-bedded and very fine-grained; in upper part, sandstone is massive and conglomeratic.	Shales may weather preferentially and may destabilize the rock column. In areas where more resistant sandstones overlie weathered shales, a block fall hazard may exist. Breathitt coals are underlain by weak clay layers. The Pennington contains clay layers (paleosols) that may also weaken the rock column. Moderate erosion resistance.	No fossils documented in park; however, there is potential for fossil plants and marine fossils. Clay layers within the Pennington are paleosols. Sandstone, shale, siltstone, conglomerate	Unit spans the depositional settings between the Breathitt Group (Pennsylvanian) and Pennington Groups (Mississippian).
MISSISSIPPIAN	Pennington Group	Pennington Group: (*Mp*) Upper part (***Mpu***) Pinnacle Overlook Sandstone (***Mpo***) Lower part (***Mpl***)	***Mp*** includes interbedded green, gray, reddish brown, thin-bedded to laminated, carbonaceous, calcareous siltstone and shale. Sandstone within ***Mp*** is of two types. The first is fine- to medium-grained, well sorted, medium- to thick-bedded, and light to medium gray; the second is fine-grained, thin-bedded, and greenish gray. Some argillaceous, olive gray limestone occurs near the base of ***Mp***. ***Mpu*** is medium to olive gray shale with some thin coal beds and underclays locally. ***Mpo*** contains fine- to coarse-grained, partly conglomeratic, massive, white to light gray sandstone grading laterally into calcareous siltstone and shale. ***Mpl*** is very fine to fine-grained sandstone with olive gray shale and siltstone interlayers.	Heterogeneous nature of ***Mp*** may render it unstable on slopes. Siltstone and shale form swales between ridges of sandstone. Unit contains shrink-and-swell clays. Limestone may be prone to dissolution, which may destabilize the rock column locally. ***Mpo*** forms cliffs, which may be prone to slope processes such as blockfall and sliding. Moderate erosion resistance.	Marine fossil fragments, fossiliferous limestone Siltstone, shale, sandstone, limestone, coal fragments Units form alternating ridges and swales in upland areas.	***Mp*** forms cliffs along the crest of Pine Mountain and Cumberland Mountain. ***Mpo*** was originally mapped as a lower unit within the Lee Formation.
		Newman Limestone: (***Mn***) Upper member (***Mnu***) Lower member (***Mnl***) ----- Lower member, Newman Limestone and Fort Payne Chert (***Mnf***) Grainger Formation (***Mg***)	***Mn*** contains upper beds (8 to 12 m [25 to 40 ft]) of olive gray shale with limestone lenses, and impure limestone overlying beds. Lower portions of ***Mn*** contain medium- to thick-bedded, fine-grained, medium gray limestone and dolomite. ***Mnu*** contains shale and limestone with some blocky claystone interbedded with limestone. ***Mnl*** contains crypto-crystalline to medium-crystalline, dense, light to dark gray limestone with some dolomitic limestone in the basal beds. ***Mnf*** consists of massive limestone; light gray, pink, or white chert; and silty dolomite. ***Mg*** contains interbedded red, green, and gray, laminated to medium-bedded siltstone and shale. ***Mnu***, ***Mnl***, and ***Mg*** mapped within the park.	Limestone and to a lesser extent, dolomite, are susceptible to dissolution and may form karst features such as caves, sinkholes, and sinking springs. Fractured blocks of ***Mn*** prone to rock fall. ***Mg*** forms steep, rubble-covered slopes associated with mass wasting. Moderate erosion resistance.	Chert may have provided tool material for American Indians. Fossiliferous (marine) limestone Limestone, dolomite, shale, oolitic zones, sparry calcite, chert nodules and layers. Gap Cave formed in *Mnu* and/or *Mnl*. ***Mg*** weathers to produce reddish green soil.	Carbonate units record longstanding marine deposition during the Mississippian. ***Mnl*** forms prominent cliff along north slope of Pine Mountain. ***Mg*** formed in the subaqueous portion of a deltaic system that prograded westward.
LOWER MISSISSIPPIAN-MIDDLE DEVONIAN		Chattanooga Shale (*MDc*)*	Unit consists of fissile to platy, brittle, carbonaceous, locally pyritic and silty, dark gray to black shale. Unit weathers to a rusty red and greenish yellow color in outcrop. Mostly poorly exposed. * The black shale of the Chattanooga Shale is now interpreted as Upper Devonian (S. Greb, geologist, Kentucky Geological Survey, written communication, May 2011).	*MDc* forms gentle colluvium-covered slopes along the sole of Pine Mountain. Associated with thrust faulting and is locally deformed. Does not provide stable foundations. Contains shrink-and-swell clays, uranium-rich minerals, and sulfides. May be responsible for radon accumulation in basements. Tends to be highly fractured in outcrop. Low erosion resistance.	Sparse conodonts, linguloid brachiopods, plant spores Shale, unit is a source rock for natural gas in the Appalachian Basin to the east of the park. Unit weathers to produce shaly, dark soils	Unit records marine conditions at the end of the Devonian when the lower part of the water column was anoxic causing great preservation of organic matter and black color. At depth, this unit is a source rock for oil and gas resources.

Gray-shaded rows indicate units included within the GIS data for Cumberland Gap National Historical Park but not mapped within the park.

Age	Group Name	Map Unit (Symbol)	Geologic Description	Geologic Issues	Geologic Features and Processes	Geologic History and Park Connections
UPPER SILURIAN		Hancock Dolomite (*Sh*)	***Sh*** contains fine-grained to very fine-grained dolomite with local limestone and coral reef zones as well as sandstone lenses.	Unit (especially limestone layers) is prone to dissolution and may form karst features such as sinking springs. Moderate erosion resistance.	Coral reef zones Dolomite, limestone, sandstone	Unit is capped by an unconformity representing missing geologic record between the Upper Silurian and Middle Devonian.
MIDDLE SILURIAN		Clinton Shale (*Sct*)	Unit contains pale olive shale; numerous, thin, greenish gray beds of siltstone; and a few conglomeratic beds of fine- to medium-grained sandstone.	Shale rich unit may weather to clay and be prone to mass wasting processes of slumping and sliding where exposed on slopes. Moderately low erosion resistance.	No fossils documented in park; however, there is potential for marine fossils Shale, siltstone, sandstone, conglomerate, oolitic hematite in 2.5 cm to 1 m (1 in. to 3.5 ft) thick beds	Unit records deep water depositional conditions present during the Middle Silurian
MIDDLE SILURIAN-LOWER SILURIAN		Rockwood Formation: (*Sr*) Upper shale member (***Sru***) Sandstone member (***Srs***) Lower shale member (***Srl***)	***Sr*** includes pale olive green shale interbedded with siltstone and thin to thick sandstone beds. Lower reaches of this unit are grayish red shale interlayered with thin-bedded sandstone. ***Sru*** contains olive gray shale with some reddish and greenish beds, siltstone, and fine-grained sandstone. ***Srs*** consists of very fine to fine-grained, thin- to thick-bedded, medium to brownish gray sandstone with some shale interbeds. ***Srs*** also contains a coarsely crystalline limestone bed as thick as 1.2 m (4 ft). ***Srl*** contains olive gray to dark greenish gray shale and a few thin sandstone beds.	Calcareous zones in ***Sr*** may weather preferentially providing zones of weakness that may fail when exposed on slopes. Moderately low to moderate erosion resistance for sandstone beds	Marine fossils Shale, siltstone, sandstone, hematitic and oolitic zones	Unit records shifting depositional environments present between the Middle and Lower Silurian.
LOWER SILURIAN		Clinch Sandstone: (*Sc*) Poor Valley Ridge Member (*Scp*) Hagan Shale Member (*Sch*)	***Sc*** contains pale olive shale concentrated in the lower third of the unit overlain by fine- to medium-grained, crossbedded, conglomeratic sandstone. ***Scp*** contains medium-grained sandstone with silty and shaly zones atop lenses of quartz-pebble conglomerate. ***Sch*** includes olive gray to brown shale, silty shale, and minor sandstone. ***Sc*** mapped within the park.	Shale rich unit may weather to clay and be prone to mass wasting processes of slumping and sliding where exposed on slopes. If the shale weathers away beneath a sandstone layer, blockfall could be a potential hazard. Moderate erosion resistance.	Brachiopods, marine fossils Shale, sandstone, conglomerate, hematite zones	Units record deposition in deep basin to nearshore environments during the Lower Silurian.
UPPER ORDOVICIAN		Sequatchie Formation (*Os*)	***Os*** consists of thin- to medium-bedded siltstone with shale and limestone, locally. Some sandstone is present in the upper part. Colors vary from grayish red, dark greenish gray to brownish and medium gray.	Limestone zones in ***Os*** may weather preferentially providing zones of weakness that may fail when exposed on slopes. Moderate erosion resistance.	No fossils documented in park; however, there is potential for marine fossils Siltstone, shale, sandstone, limestone	Units record open marine depositional settings present during the Upper Ordovician.
	Chickamauga Group	Reedsville Shale (*Or*)	***Or*** contains gray to grayish green shale with some minor gray and green siltstone interbeds. Unit grades laterally into limestone with gray sandstone lenses present locally.	Shale rich unit may weather to clay and be prone to mass wasting processes of slumping and sliding where exposed on slopes. Limestone zones in ***Or*** may weather preferentially providing zones of weakness that may fail when exposed on slopes. Moderately low erosion resistance.	Bryozoan reefs, coquinoid limestone Shale, siltstone, limestone, sandstone.	Units record deep water deposition during the Upper Ordovician.

Gray-shaded rows indicate units included within the GIS data for Cumberland Gap National Historical Park but not mapped within the park.

Age	Group Name	Map Unit (Symbol)	Geologic Description	Geologic Issues	Geologic Features and Processes	Geologic History and Park Connections
UPPER ORDOVICIAN	Chickamauga Group	Trenton Limestone (*Ot*) Eggleston Limestone (*Oe*) Hardy Creek Limestone (*Ohc*) Ben Hur Limestone (*Obh*) Woodway Limestone (*Ow*) Hurricane Bridge Limestone (*Ohb*)	***Ot*** contains medium-crystalline, medium gray limestone in beds less than 20 cm (8 in.) thick. Some very fine- to fine-grained sandstone is present in the lower layers. ***Oe*** includes very fine-grained gray limestone, calcareous shale, claystone, and bentonite beds. ***Ohc*** contains fine- to very fine-grained gray limestone and argillaceous limestone with distinctive black chert nodules. ***Obh*** is fine-grained, platy, argillaceous limestone. ***Ow*** contains very fine-grained to medium-crystalline, thin to thick beds of gray limestone. ***Ohb*** contains fine- to very fine-grained, medium to thick beds with some zones of grayish red, shaly, mudcracked limestone. ***Ot, Oe,*** and ***Ohc*** mapped within the park.	Limestone units are prone to dissolution and may form karst features such as sinking springs and dissolution conduits. Bentonite is a shrink-and-swell clay that can compromise foundations, roads, trails, and other infrastructure. Moderate erosion resistance.	Chert in upper reaches of ***Ot*** may have provided tool material for American Indians Fossil fragments, coquinoid layers, *Stromatocerium rogusum*, gastropods, *Camarncladia* Limestone, sandstone, chert, shale, bentonite, calcite "birdseyes", "marble" in ***Ohb*** ***Obh*** weathers to produce shaly residuum and calcium rich soils.	Units record longstanding carbonate depositional environment present during the Middle Ordovician within an open marine basin.
		Martin Creek, Rob Camp, and Poteet Limestone, undivided (*Omrp*) Martin Creek Limestone and Poteet Limestone, undivided (*Omp*) Martin Creek Limestone (*Omc*) Rob Camp Limestone (*Orc*) Poteet Limestone and Dot Formation, undivided (*Opd*) Poteet Limestone (*Op*) Dot Formation (*Od*)	***Omrp*** and ***Omp*** contain very fine- to medium-grained, light olive gray to brownish gray, argillaceous limestone with black chert nodules present locally. ***Omc*** consists of fine- to very fine-grained, medium- to thick-bedded, dark gray limestone with as much as 9 m (30 ft) of calcarenite in the upper beds. ***Orc*** consists of massive, light olive gray limestone. ***Opd*** contains argillaceous, light olive gray limestone in the upper beds with light olive gray limestone interlayered with yellowish gray dolomite, and pebble conglomerate in the lower beds. ***Op*** contains argillaceous yellowish limestone with dark chert nodules concentrated in the lower beds. ***Od*** includes basal beds of grayish red to yellowish gray, argillaceous, conglomeratic dolomite. Middle and upper parts contain light gray shale, and olive gray limestone.	Limestone units are prone to dissolution and may form karst features such as sinking springs and dissolution conduits. Moderate erosion resistance.	Chert may have provided tool and trade material for American Indians No fossils documented in park; however, there is potential for marine fossils Limestone, chert, white calcite, conglomerate, dolomite	Units record open marine depositional settings present during the Middle Ordovician.
LOWER ORDOVICIAN	Knox Group	Newala Dolomite and Longview Dolomite, undivided (*Onl*) Newala Dolomite (*On*) Longview Dolomite (*Ol*)	***Onl*** consists of ***On*** and ***Ol. On*** is very finely to finely crystalline, light olive gray dolomite in beds ranging from 15 cm (6 in.) to 30 cm (1 ft) thick. Some beds are grayish red. Unit also contains some fine-grained chert and matrix sandstone in the upper beds. ***Ol*** includes coarsely crystalline, light gray dolomite.	Dolomite is less soluble than limestone, but the potential for dissolution still exists. This can profoundly impact the hydrology of an area. Blockfall potential exists for these units if exposed on slopes. Moderate erosion resistance.	Chert may have provided tool and trade material for American Indians. No fossils documented in park; however, there is potential for marine fossils Dolomite, chert beds and nodules	Units record open marine depositional settings present during the Lower Ordovician.

Gray-shaded rows indicate units included within the GIS data for Cumberland Gap National Historical Park but not mapped within the park.

Age	Group Name	Map Unit (Symbol)	Geologic Description	Geologic Issues	Geologic Features and Processes	Geologic History and Park Connections
LOWER ORDOVICIAN	Knox Group	Kingsport Formation (*Ok*) Mascot Dolomite (*Oma*) Chepultepec Dolomite: (*Oc*) Upper member (*Ocu*) Lower member (*Ocl*)	***Ok*** includes medium crystalline, thick-bedded, light to medium gray dolomite with thin sandstone and grayish green silty shale interbeds near the top of the unit. ***Oma*** contains fine- to very fine-grained gray dolomite with thin sandstone lenses and masses of chert. ***Oc*** consists of fine- to medium-grained, thin- to thick-bedded, gray dolomite. ***Ocu*** contains fine- to very fine-grained gray dolomite in beds 15 cm (6 in.) to 1 m (3 ft) thick., one fine-grained sandstone bed, and chert nodules and masses in lower beds. ***Ocl*** contains gray dolomite and dolomitic sandstone in planar beds.	Carbonate cements within ***Oc*** weather preferentially causing localized portions of the unit to be friable and unstable. Moderate erosion resistance.	Chert may have provided tool and trade material for American Indians. Stromatolitic zones occur in ***Oma***. Dolomite, sandstone, chert ***Oc*** weathers to produce sandstone- or shale-rich regolith.	Units record open marine depositional settings present during the Lower Ordovician.
UPERR CAMBRIAN	Knox and Conasauga Groups	Copper Ridge Dolomite and Maynardville Limestone, undivided (*Ccrm*)	***Ccrm*** consists of fine- to medium-grained, medium- to thick-bedded, medium gray dolomite with sandy zones and chert locally. Oolitic zone present near the top of the formation.	Carbonate-rich units such as limestone and to a lesser extent dolomite are prone to dissolution and have the potential to host karst features such as dissolution conduits. Such conditions can strongly affect the hydrology of a given area. Moderate erosion resistance.	Chert may have provided tool and trade material for American Indians. Limestone, dolomite, oolitic zones, chert	Thrust faulting throughout this unit cuts off the base of the Copper Ridge Dolomite and juxtaposes it with the Maynardville Limestone.
MIDDLE CAMBRIAN	Conasauga Group	Copper Ridge Dolomite (*Ccr*) Maynardville Limestone (*Cmn*) Conasauga Shale (*Cc*)	***Ccr*** contains coarsely crystalline, olive brownish gray dolomite in irregular beds throughout the lower portion overlain by very finely to finely crystalline olive brownish gray to light gray dolomite. Lower portions of ***Cmn*** contain dark gray limestone ribboned with very finely crystalline, argillaceous olive gray dolomite. Upper beds are very finely crystalline dolomite in even beds about 15 cm (6 in.) thick. ***Cc*** contains dark greenish-gray shale with some reddish shale and dark gray limestone interbeds.	Limestone units are prone to dissolution and may form karst features such as sinking springs and dissolution conduits. Shale rich units may provide zones of weakness and could be prone to fail on slopes. Moderate to moderately low erosion resistance for shale.	Chert may have provided tool and trade material for American Indians. Limestone, dolomite, chert, conglomerate	Units record open marine depositional settings present throughout the Middle Cambrian.
		Maryville Limestone (*Cm*) Rogersville Shale (*Crg*) Rutledge Limestone (*Crt*) Pumpkin Valley Shale (*Cpv*)	***Cm*** consists of fine- to very fine-grained, bluish gray limestone with interbeds of silty dolomite, shale, flat-pebble limestone conglomerate, and oolitic zones. ***Crg*** contains olive gray to medium gray shale interlayered with lenses of siltstone and limestone. ***Crt*** contains fine- to very fine-grained, bluish gray limestone with some silty dolomitic laminae, shale zones, and flat-pebble conglomerate. ***Cpv*** consists of red, green, and gray shale with some siltstone and limestone lenses in the upper part and interbedded shale, siltstone, and limestone in the lower part.	Weathering of shale layers or dissolution of carbonate layers can create zones of instability within the rock column. Dissolution conduits within limestones can have pronounced effects on the hydrology of an area. Moderate to moderately low erosion resistance for shales.	Fossil fragments, small brachiopods Limestone, dolomite, shale, conglomerate, oolite, glauconite, white mica flakes	The Clinchport Fault cuts the top of ***Cm*** at the surface.
LOWER CAMBRIAN		Rome Formation (*Cr*)	***Cr*** contains shaly, glauconitic sandstone underlain by red, green, and gray shale, silty shale, siltstone, and sandstone. Some interbedded limestone and dolomite occurs in a bed some 15 m (50 ft) thick about 120 m (400 ft) from the top of the formation.	Shale layers can weather to clay producing zones of weakness. If resistant sandstones are undercut by the preferential weathering of shales, a blockfall hazard can exist. Moderate erosion resistance.	Sandstone, glauconite, shale, siltstone, dolomite, limestone	A thrust fault cuts off the base of this formation.

Glossary

This glossary contains brief definitions of technical geologic terms used in this report. Not all geologic terms used are referenced. For more detailed definitions or to find terms not listed here please visit: http://geomaps.wr.usgs.gov/parks/misc/glossarya.html. Definitions are based on those in the American Geological Institute Glossary of Geology (fifth edition; 2005).

absolute age. The geologic age of a fossil, rock, feature, or event in years; commonly refers to radiometrically determined ages.

accretion. The gradual addition of new land to old by the deposition of sediment or emplacement of landmasses onto the edge of a continent at a convergent margin.

active margin. A tectonically active margin where lithospheric plates come together (convergent boundary), pull apart (divergent boundary) or slide past one another (transform boundary). Typically associated with earthquakes and, in the case of convergent and divergent boundaries, volcanism. Compare to "passive margin."

alluvial fan. A fan-shaped deposit of sediment that accumulates where a hydraulically confined stream flows to a hydraulically unconfined area. Commonly out of a mountainous area into an area such as a valley or plain.

alluvium. Stream-deposited sediment.

anticline. A convex-upward ("A" shaped) fold. Older rocks are found in the center.

aquifer. A rock or sedimentary unit that is sufficiently porous that it has a capacity to hold water, sufficiently permeable to allow water to move through it, and currently saturated to some level.

arc. See "volcanic arc" and "magmatic arc."

arenite. A general term for sedimentary rocks composed of sand-sized fragments with a pure or nearly pure chemical cement and little or no matrix material between the fragments.

axis (fold). A straight line approximation of the trend of a fold which divides the two limbs of the fold. "Hinge line" is a preferred term.

basement. The undifferentiated rocks, commonly igneous and metamorphic, that underlie rocks exposed at the surface.

basin (structural). A doubly plunging syncline in which rocks dip inward from all sides.

basin (sedimentary). Any depression, from continental to local scales, into which sediments are deposited.

bed. The smallest sedimentary strata unit, commonly ranging in thickness from one centimeter to a meter or two and distinguishable from beds above and below.

bedding. Depositional layering or stratification of sediments.

bedrock. A general term for the rock that underlies soil or other unconsolidated, surficial material.

block (fault). A crustal unit bounded by faults, either completely or in part.

breccia. A coarse-grained, generally unsorted sedimentary rock consisting of cemented angular clasts greater than 2 mm (0.08 in).

brittle. Describes a rock that fractures (breaks) before sustaining deformation.

calcareous. Describes rock or sediment that contains the mineral calcium carbonate (CaCO3).

calcite. A common rock-forming mineral: $CaCO_3$ (calcium carbonate).

carbonaceous. Describes a rock or sediment with considerable carbon content, especially organics, hydrocarbons, or coal.

carbonate. A mineral that has CO3-2 as its essential component (e.g., calcite and aragonite).

carbonate rock. A rock consisting chiefly of carbonate minerals (e.g., limestone, dolomite, or carbonatite).

cementation. Chemical precipitation of material into pores between grains that bind the grains into rock.

chemical sediment. A sediment precipitated directly from solution (also called nonclastic).

chemical weathering. Chemical breakdown of minerals at Earth's surface via reaction with water, air, or dissolved substances; commonly results in a change in chemical composition more stable in the current environment.

chert. A extremely hard sedimentary rock with conchoidal (smooth curved surface) fracturing. It consists chiefly of interlocking crystals of quartz Also called "flint."

clast. An individual grain or rock fragment in a sedimentary rock, produced by the physical disintegration of a larger rock mass.

clastic. Describes rock or sediment made of fragments of pre-existing rocks (clasts).

clay. Can be used to refer to clay minerals or as a sedimentary fragment size classification (less than 1/256 mm [0.00015 in]).

claystone. Lithified clay having the texture and composition of shale but lacking shale's fine layering and fissility (characteristic splitting into thin layers).

colluvium. A general term for any loose, heterogeneous, and incoherent mass of soil material and/or rock fragments deposited through the action of surface runoff (rainwash, sheetwash) or slow continuous downslope creep.

concordant. Strata with contacts parallel to the orientation of adjacent strata.

concretion. A hard, compact aggregate of mineral matter, subspherical to irregular in shape; formed by precipitation from water solution around a nucleus such as shell or bone in a sedimentary or pyroclastic rock. Concretions are generally different in composition from the rocks in which they occur.

conglomerate. A coarse-grained, generally unsorted, sedimentary rock consisting of cemented, rounded clasts larger than 2 mm (0.08 in).

continental crust. Crustal rocks rich in silica and alumina that underlie the continents; ranging in thickness from 35 km (22 mi) to 60 km (37 mi) under mountain ranges.

convergent boundary. A plate boundary where two tectonic plates are colliding.

crossbed. A single bed, inclined at an angle to the main planes of stratification; frequently used to determine flow directions.

craton. The relatively old and geologically stable interior of a continent.

creep. The slow, imperceptible downslope movement of mineral, rock, and soil particles under gravity.

crinoid. A marine invertebrate (echinoderm) that uses a stalk to attach itself to a substrate. "Arms" are used to capture food. Rare today, they were very common in the Paleozoic. Crinoids are also called "sea lilies."

cross-bedding. Uniform to highly varied sets of inclined sedimentary beds deposited by wind or water that indicate flow conditions such as water flow direction and depth.

cross section. A graphical interpretation of geology, structure, and/or stratigraphy in the third (vertical) dimension based on mapped and measured geological extents and attitudes depicted in a vertically oriented plane.

crust. Earth's outermost compositional shell, 10 to 40 km (6 to 25 mi) thick, consisting predominantly of relatively low-density silicate minerals (also see "oceanic crust" and "continental crust").

crystalline. Describes a regular, orderly, repeating geometric structural arrangement of atoms.

cutbank. A steep, bare slope formed by lateral erosion of a stream.

debris flow. A moving mass of rock fragments, soil, and mud, in which more than half the particles of which are larger than sand size.

décollement. A large-displacement (kilometers to tens of kilometers), shallowly-dipping to sub-horizontal fault or shear zone.

deformation. A general term for the process of faulting, folding, and shearing of rocks as a result of various Earth forces such as compression (pushing together) and extension (pulling apart).

delta. A sediment wedge deposited where a stream flows into a lake or sea.

detachment fault. Synonym for décollement. Widely used for a regionally extensive, gently dipping normal fault that is commonly associated with extension in a metamorphic core complex.

detritus. A collective term for lose rock and mineral material that is worn off or removed by mechanical means.

dip. The angle between a bed or other geologic surface and horizontal.

dip-slip fault. A fault with measurable offset where the relative movement is parallel to the dip of the fault.

discordant. Describes contacts between strata that cut across or are set at an angle to the orientation of adjacent rocks.

divergent boundary. An active boundary where tectonic plates are moving apart (e.g., a spreading ridge or continental rift zone).

doline. A type of sinkhole, or a karst collapse feature.

dolomite. A carbonate sedimentary rock of which more than 50% by weight or by areal percentages under the microscope consists of the mineral dolomite (calcium-magnesium carbonate).

dolomitic. Describes a dolomite-bearing rock, or a rock containing dolomite.

downcutting. Stream erosion process in which the cutting is directed in primarily downward, as opposed to lateral erosion.

drainage basin. The total area from which a stream system receives or drains precipitation runoff.

escarpment. A steep cliff or topographic step resulting from vertical displacement on a fault or by mass movement. Also called a "scarp."

evaporite. A sedimentary rock composed primarily of minerals produced from a saline solution as a result of extensive or total evaporation of the solvent (usually water).

extension. A type of strain resulting from forces "pulling apart." Opposite of compression.

facies (sedimentary). The depositional or environmental conditions reflected in the sedimentary structures, textures, mineralogy, fossils, etc. of a sedimentary rock.

fan delta. An alluvial fan that builds into a standing body of water. This landform differs from a delta in that a fan delta is next to a highland and typically forms at an active margin.

fanglomerate. A sedimentary rock of heterogeneous materials that were originally deposited in an alluvial fan and have since been cemented into solid rock.

fault. A break in rock along which relative movement has occurred between the two sides.

floodplain. The surface or strip of relatively smooth land adjacent to a river channel and formed by the river. Covered with water when the river overflows its banks.

fold. A curve or bend of an originally flat or planar structure such as rock strata, bedding planes, or foliation that is usually a product of deformation.

foliation. A preferred arrangement of crystal planes in minerals. In metamorphic rocks, the term commonly refers to a parallel orientation of planar minerals such as micas.

footwall. The mass of rock beneath a fault surface (also see "hanging wall").

formation. Fundamental rock-stratigraphic unit that is mappable, lithologically distinct from adjoining strata, and has definable upper and lower contacts.

fracture. Irregular breakage of a mineral; also any break in a rock (e.g., crack, joint, or fault).

frost wedging. The breakup of rock due to the expansion of water freezing in fractures.

geology. The study of Earth including its origin, history, physical processes, components, and morphology.

glauconite. A green mineral, closely related to the micas. It is an indicator of very slow sedimentation.

hanging wall. The mass of rock above a fault surface (also see "footwall").

hinge line. A line or boundary between a stable region and one undergoing upward or downward movement.

hydraulic conductivity. Measure of permeability coefficient.

hydrogeologic. Refers to the geologic influences on groundwater and surface water composition, movement and distribution.

incision. The process whereby a downward-eroding stream deepens its channel or produces a narrow, steep-walled valley.

island arc. A line or arc of volcanic islands formed over and parallel to a subduction zone.

isoclinal. Describes a fold with parallel limbs.

joint. A break in rock without relative movement of rocks on either side of the fracture surface.

karst topography. Topography characterized by abundant sinkholes and caverns formed by the dissolution of calcareous rocks.

karst valley. A closed depression formed by the coalescence of several sinkholes.

karst window. A collapse sinkhole opening into a cave.

lamination. Very thin, parallel layers.

landslide. Any process or landform resulting from rapid, gravity-driven mass movement.

left lateral fault. A strike slip fault on which the side opposite the observer has been displaced to the left Synonymous with "sinistral fault."

lignite. A brownish-black coal that is intermediate in coalification between peat and subbituminous coal.

limb. Either side of a structural fold.

limestone. A sedimentary rock consisting chiefly of calcium carbonate, primarily in the form of the mineral calcite.

lineament. Any relatively straight surface feature that can be identified via observation, mapping, or remote sensing, often reflects crustal structure.

lithic. A sedimentary rock or pyroclastic deposit that contains abundant fragments of previously formed rocks.

lithification. The conversion of sediment into solid rock.

lithify. To change to stone or to petrify; especially to consolidate from a loose sediment to a solid rock through compaction and cementation.

lithology. The physical description or classification of a rock or rock unit based on characters such as its color, mineral composition, and grain size.

marine terrace. A narrow coastal strip of deposited material, sloping gently seaward.

marker bed. A distinctive layer used to trace a geologic unit from one geographic location to another.

mass wasting. A general term for the downslope movement of soil and rock material under the direct influence of gravity.

matrix. The fine grained material between coarse (larger) grains in igneous rocks or poorly sorted clastic sediments or rocks. Also refers to rock or sediment in which a fossil is embedded.

mechanical weathering. The physical breakup of rocks without change in composition. Synonymous with "physical weathering."

megabreccia. A term for a coarse breccia containing individual blocks as much as 400 m (1,300 ft) long.

member. A lithostratigraphic unit with definable contacts; a member subdivides a formation.

mineral. A naturally occurring, inorganic crystalline solid with a definite chemical composition or compositional range.

nonconformity. An erosional surface preserved in strata in which crystalline igneous or metamorphic rocks underlie sedimentary rocks.

normal fault. A dip-slip fault in which the hanging wall moves down relative to the footwall.

oblique fault. A fault in which motion includes both dip-slip and strike-slip components (also see "dip-slip fault" and "strike-slip fault").

oceanic crust. Earth's crust formed at spreading ridges that underlies the ocean basins. Oceanic crust is 6 to 7 km (3 to 4 miles) thick and generally of basaltic composition.

oolite. A sedimentary rock, usually limestone, made of ooliths—round or oval grains formed by accretion around a nucleus of shell fragment, algal pellet, or sand grain. These laminated grains can reach diameters of 2 mm (0.08 in), but 0.5–1 mm (0.02–0.04 in) is common.

orogeny. A mountain-building event.

ostracode. Any aquatic crustacean belonging to the subclass Ostracoda, characterized by a two-valved (shelled), generally calcified carapace with a hinge along the dorsal margin. Most ostracodes are of microscopic size.

outcrop. Any part of a rock mass or formation that is exposed or "crops out" at Earth's surface.

overbank deposit. Alluvium deposited outside a stream channel during flooding.

paleontology. The study of the life and chronology of Earth's geologic past based on the fossil record.

Pangaea. A theoretical, single supercontinent that existed during the Permian and Triassic periods.

passive margin. A margin where no plate-scale tectonism is taking place; plates are not converging, diverging, or sliding past one another. An example is the east coast of North America. (also see "active margin").

pebble. Generally, small rounded rock particles from 4 to 64 mm (0.16 to 2.52 in) in diameter.

permeability. A measure of the relative ease with which fluids move through the pore spaces of rocks or sediments.

plate tectonics. The concept that the lithosphere is broken up into a series of rigid plates that move over Earth's surface above a more fluid asthenosphere.

plateau. A broad, flat-topped topographic high (terrestrial or marine) of great extent and elevation above the surrounding plains, canyons, or valleys.

platform. Any level or nearly-level surface, ranging in size from a terrace or bench to a plateau or peneplain.

porosity. The proportion of void space (e.g., pores or voids) in a volume of rock or sediment deposit.

progradation. The seaward building of land area due to sedimentary deposition.

pull-apart basin. A topographic depression created by an extensional bend or extensional overstep along a strike-slip fault.

quartz arenite. A sandstone composed of greater than 90% detrital quartz, with limited amounts of other mineral clasts (e.g. feldspar) and matrix.

quartzite. Metamorphosed quartz sandstone.

radioactivity. The spontaneous decay or breakdown of unstable atomic nuclei.

radiometric age. An age expressed in years and calculated from the quantitative determination of radioactive elements and their decay products.

recharge. Infiltration processes that replenish groundwater.

regolith. General term for the layer of rock debris, organic matter, and soil that commonly forms the land surface and overlies most bedrock.

regression. A long-term seaward retreat of the shoreline or relative fall of sea level.

relative dating. Determining the chronological placement of rocks, events, or fossils with respect to the geologic time scale and without reference to their numerical age.

reverse fault. A contractional high-angle (greater than 45°) dip-slip fault in which the hanging wall moves up relative to the footwall (also see "thrust fault").

rift. A region of crust where extension results in formation of many related normal faults, often associated with volcanic activity.

rift valley. A depression formed by grabens along the crest of an oceanic spreading ridge or in a continental rift zone.

ripple marks. The undulating, approximately parallel and usually small-scale ridge pattern formed on sediment by the flow of wind or water.

riprap. A layer of large, durable, broken rock fragments irregularly thrown together in an attempt to prevent erosion by waves or currents and thereby preserve the shape of a surface, slope, or underlying structure.

rock. A solid, cohesive aggregate of one or more minerals.

rock fall. Mass wasting process where rocks are dislodged and move downslope rapidly; it is the fastest mass wasting process.

roundness. The relative amount of curvature of the "corners" of a sediment grain.

sand. A clastic particle smaller than a granule and larger than a silt grain, having a diameter in the range of 1/16 mm (0.0025 in) to 2 mm (0.08 in).

sandstone. Clastic sedimentary rock of predominantly sand-sized grains.

sapping. The undercutting of a cliff by erosion of softer underlying rock layers.

scarp. A steep cliff or topographic step resulting from displacement on a fault, or by mass movement, or erosion. Also called an "escarpment."

sediment. An eroded and deposited, unconsolidated accumulation of rock and mineral fragments.

sedimentary rock. A consolidated and lithified rock consisting of clastic and/or chemical sediment(s). One of the three main classes of rocks—igneous, metamorphic, and sedimentary.

sequence. A major informal rock-stratigraphic unit that is traceable over large areas and defined by a sediments associated with a major sea level transgression-regression.

shale. A clastic sedimentary rock made of clay-sized particles that exhibit parallel splitting properties.

silt. Clastic sedimentary material intermediate in size between fine-grained sand and coarse clay (1/256 to 1/16 mm [0.00015 to 0.002 in]).

siltstone. A variably lithified sedimentary rock composed of silt-sized grains.

slope. The inclined surface of any geomorphic feature or measurement thereof. Synonymous with "gradient."

slump. A generally large, coherent mass movement with a concave-up failure surface and subsequent backward rotation relative to the slope.

soil. Surface accumulation of weathered rock and organic matter capable of supporting plant growth and often overlying the parent material from which it formed.

speleothem. Any secondary mineral deposit that forms in a cave.

spring. A site where water issues from the surface due to the intersection of the water table with the ground surface.

strata. Tabular or sheet-like masses or distinct layers of rock.

stratification. The accumulation, or layering of sedimentary rocks in strata. Tabular, or planar, stratification refers to essentially parallel surfaces. Cross-stratification refers to strata inclined at an angle to the main stratification.

stratigraphy. The geologic study of the origin, occurrence, distribution, classification, correlation, and age of rock layers, especially sedimentary rocks.

stream. Any body of water moving under gravity flow in a clearly confined channel.

stream channel. A long, narrow depression shaped by the concentrated flow of a stream and covered continuously or periodically by water.

stream terrace. Step-like benches surrounding the present floodplain of a stream due to dissection of previous flood plain(s), stream bed(s), and/or valley floor(s).

strike. The compass direction of the line of intersection of an inclined surface with a horizontal plane.

strike-slip fault. A fault with measurable offset where the relative movement is parallel to the strike of the fault. Said to be "sinistral" (left-lateral) if relative motion of the block opposite the observer appears to be to the left. "Dextral" (right-lateral) describes relative motion to the right.

structural geology. The branch of geology that deals with the description, representation, and analysis of structures, chiefly on a moderate to small scale. The subject is similar to tectonics, but the latter is generally used for the broader regional or historical phases.

structure. The attitude and relative positions of the rock masses of an area resulting from such processes as faulting, folding, and igneous intrusions.

subbituminous. A black coal, intermediate in rank between lignite and bituminous coal. It is distinguished from lignite by higher carbon and lower moisture content.

subsidence. The gradual sinking or depression of part of Earth's surface.

syncline. A downward curving (concave up) fold with layers that dip inward; the core of the syncline contains the stratigraphically-younger rocks.

system (stratigraphy). The group of rocks formed during a period of geologic time.

talus. Rock fragments, usually coarse and angular, lying at the base of a cliff or steep slope from which they have been derived.

tectonic. Relating to large-scale movement and deformation of Earth's crust.

tectonics. The geologic study of the broad structural architecture and deformational processes of the lithosphere and asthenosphere.

tempestite. A storm deposit consisting of sandy layers, showing evidence of violent disturbance of pre-existing sediments followed by their rapid redeposition, all in a shallow-water environment, but deeper than fair-weather wave base..

terrace. A relatively level bench or steplike surface breaking the continuity of a slope (see "marine terrace" and "stream terrace").

terrestrial. Relating to land, Earth, or its inhabitants.

thrust fault. A contractional dip-slip fault with a shallowly dipping fault surface (less than 45°) where the hanging wall moves up and over relative to the footwall.

topography. The general morphology of Earth's surface, including relief and locations of natural and anthropogenic features.

trace (fault). The exposed intersection of a fault with Earth's surface.

trace fossil. Tracks, trails, burrows, coprolites (dung), etc., that preserve evidence of organisms' life activities, rather than the organisms themselves.

transgression. Landward migration of the sea as a result of a relative rise in sea level.

trend. The direction or azimuth of elongation of a linear geologic feature.

type locality. The geographic location where a stratigraphic unit (or fossil) is well displayed, formally defined, and derives its name. The place of original description.

unconformity. An erosional or non-depositional surface bounded on one or both sides by sedimentary strata that marks a period of missing time.

undercutting. The removal of material at the base of a steep slope or cliff or other exposed rock by the erosive action of falling or running water (such as a meandering stream), of sand-laden wind in the desert, or of waves along the coast.

uplift. A structurally high area in the crust, produced by movement that raises the rocks.

volcanic. Describes anything related to volcanoes. Can refer to igneous rock crystallized at or near Earth's surface (e.g., lava).

volcanic arc. A commonly curved, linear, zone of volcanoes above a subduction zone.

water table. The upper surface of the saturated zone; the zone of rock in an aquifer saturated with water.

weathering. The physical, chemical, and biological processes by which rock is broken down.

Literature Cited

This section lists references cited in this report. A more complete geologic bibliography is available from the National Park Service Geologic Resources Division.

Abramson, L. W. 1993. Geotechnical exploration of complex tunnel sites. Pages 117–123 in Fickies, R. H., editor. Geologic complexities in the highway environment; proceedings of the 42nd annual highway geology symposium. New York State Geological Survey, Albany, New York, USA.

Andrews, W. 2004. Kentucky's landscape and the Civil War campaigns for Kentucky, 1861-1862. Geological Society of America Abstracts with Programs 36(2):76.

Andrews, W. M., Jr. 1998. Some thoughts on the historical significance of Pine Mountain and Pound Gap. Annual Field Conference of the Kentucky Society of Professional Geologists 1998:128–129.

Ashley, G. H. 1904. The Cumberland Gap coal field. Mining Magazine (London) 10:94–100.

Ashley, G. H. and L. C. Glenn. 1906. Geology and mineral resources of part of the Cumberland Gap coal field, Kentucky. Professional Paper 49. U.S. Geological Survey, Reston, Virginia, USA.

Brent, W. B. 1988. Geologic Map and Mineral Resources Summary of the Back Valley Quadrangle, Tennessee (scale 1:24,000). GQ-161 SE. Tennessee Division of Geology, Nashville, Tennessee, USA.

Chapman, M. C., J. W. Munsey, S. C. Whisner, and J. Whisner. 2002. The eastern Tennessee seismic zone: small earthquakes illuminating major basement faults? Geologic Society of America Abstracts with Programs. http://gsa.confex.com/gsa/2002NC/finalprogram/abstract_32405.htm. Accessed 31 December 2010.

Chestnut, D. R. 1992. Stratigraphic and structural framework of the Carboniferous rocks of the central Appalachian Basin in Kentucky. Series 11, Bulletin 3. Kentucky Geological Survey, Lexington, Kentucky, USA.

Clark, G. M., H. H. Mills, J. R. Wagner, and M. A. Gibson. 2002. SE MAPS in Tennessee; strategies and currently developed geologic sites in the Great Smoky Mountains and Cumberland Plateau regions. Geological Society of America Abstracts with Programs 32 (7):349.

Clark, L. M., E. Whitehouse, and C. J. Webb. 2007. A deeper insight to Hg bioaccumulation in the bat population in Kentucky and Tennessee. Geological Society of America Abstracts with Programs 39 (6):328.

Conley, T. J. 2003. Spatial database of the Kayjay quadrangle and part of the Fork Ridge quadrangle, Bell and Knox Counties, Kentucky (scale 1:24,000). Digitally Vectorized Geological Quadrangle DVGQ-12_1505. Kentucky Geological Survey, Lexington, Kentucky, USA.

Crawford, M. M. 2003. Spatial database of the Rose Hill quadrangle, Harlan County, Kentucky (scale 1:24,000). Digitally Vectorized Geological Quadrangle DVGQ-12_1121. Kentucky Geological Survey, Lexington, Kentucky, USA.

Crawford, M., R. A. Olson, R. S. Toomey, and L. J. Scoggins. 2008. A new resource for the geology of Mammoth Cave National Park. Geological Society of America Abstracts with Programs 40(5):67.

Crockett, M. 2005. Gap cave exploration by Cave Research Foundation Cumberland Gap. Journal of Cave and Karst Studies 67(3):198.

Currens, J. C. 2001. Generalized Block Diagram of the Pine Mountain Karst. Map and Chart 18, Series XII, 2001. Kentucky Geological Survey, Lexington, Kentucky, USA.

Davis, M. K. 1915. Topographic problems in the Cumberland Gap area. Master's thesis. University of Wisconsin at Madison, Madison, Wisconsin, USA.

Dean, C. S. 1989. Geology of the Cumberland Gap area as interpreted from the pilot bore of the Federal Highway Administration. Pages 4–9 in Moshier, S. O., editor. Annual Field Conference of the Geological Society of Kentucky, Kentucky Geological Survey, Lexington, Kentucky, USA.

Driese, S. G., leader. 1988. Field trip stops; day 2. Pages 120–135 in Driese, S. G. and D. Walker, editors. Depositional history of Paleozoic sequences; Southern Appalachians. Studies in Geology 19. University of Tennessee, Department of Geological Sciences, Knoxville, Tennessee, USA.

Energy and Minerals Section, Kentucky Geological Survey, University of Kentucky, 10-May-2005, kyog83v10: Kentucky Oil and Gas Well Data, NAD 83 Version 10. Kentucky Geological Survey, Lexington, Kentucky, USA.

Englund, K. J. 1964. Geology of the Middlesboro South quadrangle, Tennessee-Kentucky-Virginia (scale 1:24,000). GQ-301. U.S. Geological Survey, Reston, Virginia, USA.

Englund, K. J. 1964. Geology of the Middlesboro South Quadrangle, Tennessee-Kentucky-Virginia (scale 1:24,000). Geologic Quadrangle Map GQ-0301. U.S. Geological Survey, Reston, Virginia, USA.

Englund, K. J. and L. D. Harris. 1961. Geologic features of the Cumberland Gap area, Kentucky, Tennessee, and Virginia. Geological Society of Kentucky, Kentucky Geological Survey, Lexington, Kentucky, USA.

Englund, K. J. and L. D. Harris. 1961. Geologic features of the Cumberland Gap area, Kentucky, Tennessee, and Virginia. Geological Society of Kentucky, Field Trip 1961. Kentucky Geological Survey, Lexington, Kentucky, USA

Englund, K. J., E. R. Landis, and H. L. Smith. 1963. Geology of the Varilla quadrangle, Kentucky-Virginia (scale 1:24,000). GQ-190. U.S. Geological Survey, Reston, Virginia, USA.

Englund, K. J., H. L. Smith, L. D. Harris, and J. G. Stephens. 1963. Geology of the Ewing quadrangle, Kentucky and Virginia (scale 1:24,000). Map 1142-B. U.S. Geological Survey, Reston, Virginia, USA.

Englund, K. J., J. B. Roen, and A. O. Delaney. 1964. Geology of the Middlesboro North quadrangle, Kentucky (scale 1:24,000). GQ-300. U.S. Geological Survey, Reston, Virginia, USA.

Englund, K. J., R. E. Thomas, and J. B. Roen. 1993. Geology of the Cumberland Gap area, Kentucky, Tennessee, and Virginia. AAPG Bulletin 77 (8):1468.

Englund, K. J., R. E. Thomas, and J. B. Roen. 1994. Geology of the Cumberland Gap area, Kentucky, Tennessee, and Virginia. Pages 38–42 in Schultz, A. P. and E. K. Rader, editors. Studies in eastern energy and the environment; AAPG Eastern Section special volume 132. Virginia Division of Mineral Resources, Charlottesville, Virginia, USA

Ettensohn, F. R. and D. M. Bliefnick. 1982. Conodonts from a section of upper Newman Limestone and Pennington Formation (middle and upper Chester), northeastern Kentucky. Journal of Paleontology 56:1482–1488.

Environmental Protection Agency (EPA). 1993. EPA's Map of Radon Zones: Tennessee. 402-R-93-062. http://epis.epa.gov/Exe/ZyPURL.cgi?Dockey=000008KD.txt. Accessed 25 May 2010.

Filer, J. K. and J. M. Dennison. 1998. Reference stratigraphic cross-sections of Devonian Catskill clastic wedge in the south-central Appalachian Basin. Geological Society of America Abstracts with Programs 30 (7):337.

Greb, S. F. 2006. Fluvial-estuarine channels in the Paragon Formation and Pennington Group, Upper Mississippian, eastern Kentucky. Geological Society of America Abstracts with Programs 38(4):5.

Greco, D. C. 2006. Evaulation of geohazards, Cumberland Gap National Historical Park Kentucky. Trip Report. National Park Service, Geologic Resources Division, Denver, Colorado, USA. On file at GRD and park.

Gregory, M. A., R. N. Xedos, and P. D. Howell. 1999. Geology of the Battle of Perryville; using the World Wide Web to link geology and history. Geological Society of America Abstracts with Programs 31 (3):17.

Harris, A. G., Tuttle, E., and S. D. Tuttle. 1997. Geology of National Parks. Kendall/Hunt Publishing Company, Dubuque, Iowa, USA.

Harris, L. D. 1965. Geologic map of the Wheeler quadrangle, Claiborne County, Tennessee and Lee County, Virginia (scale 1:24,000). GQ-435. U.S. Geological Survey, Reston, Virginia, USA.

Harris, L. D., J. G. Stephens, and R. L. Miller. 1962. Geology of the Coleman Gap quadrangle, Tennessee and Virginia (scale 1:24,000). GQ-188. U.S. Geological Survey, Reston, Virginia, USA.

Henry, D. and M. Crockett. 2004. Cumberland Gap Cave; Cumberland Gap National Historical Park. Journal of Cave and Karst Studies 66(3):118.

Hunt-Foster, R., J. P. Kenworthy, V. L. Santucci, T. Connors, and T. L. Thornberry-Ehrlich. 2009. Paleontological resource inventory and monitoring—Cumberland Piedmont Network. Natural Resource Technical Report NPS/NRPC/NRR—2009/235. National Park Service, Fort Collins, Colorado, USA.

Johnson, T. L. 2003. Spatial database of the Varilla quadrangle, Kentucky-Virginia (scale 1:24,000). Digitally Vectorized Geological Quadrangle DVGQ-12_190. Kentucky Geological Survey, Lexington, Kentucky, USA.

Kentucky Department for Energy Development and Independence. 2010. Kentucky Energy Profile 2010. Kentucky Department for Energy Development and Independence, Frankfurt, Kentucky, USA. http://energy.ky.gov/Documents/Kentucky%20Energy%20Profile,%202010.pdf (accessed 28 September 2011).

Kentucky Geological Survey. 2006. Groundwater Contamination in Karst. University of Kentucky, Lexington, Kentucky, USA. http://www.uky.edu/KGS/water/general/karst/gwvulnerability.htm. Accessed 2 January 2011.

Kohl, M. S. and C. R.Sykes. 1991. Geologic Map and Mineral Resources Summary of the Fork Ridge Quadrangle, Tennessee. (scale 1:24,000). GQ-144 SE. Tennessee Division of Geology, Nashville, Tennessee, USA.

Krakow, J. L. 1987. Location of the Wilderness Road at Cumberland Gap National Historical Park/Kentucky, Virginia, Tennessee. National Park Service, Denver, Colorado, USA.

Leary, R. M. 1989. Description of the Cumberland Mountain Tunnel Project. Pages 3–4 in Moshier, S. O., editor. Cumberland Mountain; the inside story. Annual field conference of the Geological Society of Kentucky. Kentucky, USA.

Lord, M. L., D. Germanoski, and N. E. Allmendinger. 2009. Fluvial geomorphology: Monitoring stream systems in response to a changing environment. Pages 69–103 in R. Young and L. Norby, editors. Geological Monitoring. Geological Society of America, Boulder, Colorado, USA. Online. http://nature.nps.gov/geology/monitoring/fluvial.cfm. Accessed 19 September 2011.

Luckett, W. W. 1964. Cumberland Gap National Historical Park. Tennessee Historical Quarterly XXIII(4). The Tennessee Historical Society. http://www.nps.gov/history/history/online_books/cuga/luckett/index.htm. Accessed 23 December 2010.

Maughan, E. K. and J. F. Tazelaar. 1973. Geologic map of part of the Rose Hill quadrangle, Harlan County, Kentucky (scale 1:24,000). GQ-1121. U.S. Geological Survey, Reston, Virginia, USA.

McCoy, C. 1996. Efforts to protect Cumberland Gap from coal mining hit pay dirt. in 1996 Natural Resource Year in Review. http://www.nature.nps.gov/yearinreview/yr_rvw96/chapter6/tcumbgap.htm. Accessed 3 December 2010.

McFarlan, A. C. 1958. Behind the scenery in Kentucky. Special Publication 10. Kentucky Geological Survey, Lexington, Kentucky, USA.

Milam, K. A., J. Evenick, and B. Deane, eds. 2005. Field Guide to the Middlesboro and Flynn Creek Impact Structures. Impact Field Studies Group, Knoxville, Tennessee, USA.

Moshier, S. O. 1989. A brief history of the Cumberland Gap. Pages 2–3 in Moshier, S. O., editor. Cumberland Mountain; the inside story. Annual field conference of the Geological Society of Kentucky. Kentucky, USA.

Mullins, J. E. 2003. Spatial database of the Ewing quadrangle, Kentucky-Virginia (scale 1:24,000). Digitally Vectorized Geological Quadrangle DVGQ-12_172. Kentucky Geological Survey, Lexington, Kentucky, USA.

National Park Service. 2010. Cumberland Gap National Historical Park: Guided tours. http://www.nps.gov/cuga/planyourvisit/guidedtours.htm. Accessed 26 December 2010.

Palmer, A. N. 1981. A geological guide to Mammoth Cave National Park. Zephyrus Press, Teaneck, New Jersey, USA.

Petersen, M. D., A. D. Frankel, S. C. Harmsen, C. S. Mueller, K. M. Haller, R. L. Wheeler, R. L. Wesson, Y. Zeng, O. S. Boyd, D. M. Perkins, N. Luco, E. H. Field, C. J. Wills, and K. S. Rukstales. 2008a. 2008 United States National Seismic Hazard Maps. Fact Sheet 2008-3018. U.S. Geological Survey, Reston, Virginia, USA. http://pubs.usgs.gov/fs/2008/3018/. Accessed 30 December 2010.

Petersen, M. D., A. D. Frankel, S. C. Harmsen, C. S. Mueller, K. M. Haller, R. L. Wheeler, R. L. Wesson, Y. Zeng, O. S. Boyd, D. M. Perkins, N. Luco, E. H. Field, C. J. Wills, and K. S. Rukstales. 2008b. Documentation for the 2008 Update of the United States National Seismic Hazard Maps. Open-File Report 2008–1128. U.S. Geological Survey, Reston, Virginia, USA. http://pubs.usgs.gov/of/2008/1128/. Accessed 31 December 2010.

Ray, J. A., and J. C. Currens. 1998. Mapped Karst Ground-Water Basins in the Beaver Dam 30 x 60 Minute Quadrangle. Scale 1:100,000. Lexington, KY: Kentucky Geological Survey.

Rice, C. L. and E. K. Maughan. 1978. Geologic map of the Kayjay quadrangle and part of the Fork Ridge quadrangle, Bell and Knox Counties, Kentucky (scale 1:24,000). GQ-1505. U.S. Geological Survey, Reston, Virginia, USA.

Rich, J. L. 1933. Physiography and structure at Cumberland Gap. Geological Society of America Bulletin 44 (6):1219–1236.

Santucci, V. L., J. Kenworthy, and R. Kerbo. 2001. An inventory of paleontological resources associated with National Park Service caves. Geologic Resources Division Technical Report, NPS/NRGRD/GRDTR-01/02. Online. http://nature.nps.gov/geology/paleontology/pub/cavepaleo.pdf. Accessed 1 May 2010.

Santucci, V. L., J. P. Kenworthy, and A. L. Mims. 2009. Monitoring in situ paleontological resources. Pages 189-204 in R. Young and L. Norby, editors. Geological Monitoring. Geological Society of America, Boulder, Colorado, USA. http://nature.nps.gov/geology/monitoring/paleo.cfm. Accessed 19 September 2011.

Scanlon, B. R., and J. Thrailkill. 1987. Chemical similarities among physically distinct spring types in a karst terrain. Journal of Hydrology 89(3–4):259–279.

Smith, R., R. Olson, B. Carson, and J. Meiman. 1997. Radon Monitoring at Mammoth Cave National Park: An Interim Report. In Proceedings of the Sixth Annual Mammoth Cave National Park Science Conference: 99–110.

Southworth, S., D. K. Brezinski, R. C. Orndorff, P. G. Chirico, and K. M. Lagueux. 2001. A—Geologic map and GIS files (disc 1); B—Geologic report and figures (disc 2). In Geology of the Chesapeake and Ohio Canal National Historical Park and Potomac River Corridor, District of Columbia, Maryland, West Virginia, and Virginia. Open-File Report OF 01-0188. U.S. Geological Survey, Reston, Virginia, USA.

Sparks, T. N. and J. R. Lambert. 2003. Spatial database of the Middlesboro North quadrangle, Kentucky (scale 1:24,000). Digitally Vectorized Geological Quadrangle DVGQ-12_1663. Kentucky Geological Survey, Lexington, Kentucky, USA.

Thompson, M. F. 2003. Spatial database of the Middlesboro South quadrangle, Tennessee-Kentucky-Virginia (scale 1:24,000). Digitally Vectorized Geological Quadrangle DVGQ-12_301. Kentucky Geological Survey, Lexington, Kentucky, USA.

Thornberry-Ehrlich, T. L. 2008. Geologic Resource Evaluation [Inventory] Scoping Summary, Cumberland Gap National Historical Park. National Park Service, Geologic Resources Division, Denver, Colorado, USA. Online. http://www.nature.nps.gov/geology/inventory/publications/s_summaries/CUGA_GRI_scoping_summary_2008_11_27.pdf. Accessed 1 May 2010.

Toomey III, R. S. 2009. Geological monitoring of caves and associated landscapes. Pages 27–46 in R. Young and L. Norby, editors. Geological Monitoring. Geological Society of America, Boulder, Colorado, USA. http://nature.nps.gov/geology/monitoring/cavekarst.cfm. Accessed 19 September 2011.

Unrau, H. D. 2002. Restoration of Historic Features: Cumberland Gap National Historical Park. National Park Service, Denver, Colorado, USA.

Walker, G. L., D. Ballinger, U. Matthes, and D. Dobson. 2007. Physical variables and community structure of the White Rocks cliff system, Cumberland Gap National Historical Park. Appalachian State University, Boone, North Carolina, USA. Unpublished report. On file at park.

Watson, A E. and F. R. Ettensohn. 1991. Nature and origin of the Mississippian-Pennsylvanian unconformity in the Cumberland Gap area. Geological Society of America Abstracts with Programs 23 (1):146.

Whisonant, R. C., P. S. Sethi, K. K. Cecil, P. L. Newbill, and L. L. Combs. 2002. Connecting geology and human history; examples from a multimedia CD-ROM series concerning the geology of Virginia. Geological Society of America Abstracts with Programs 34 (2):105.

Wieczorek, TG. F. and J. B. Snyder. 2009. Monitoring slope movements. Pages 245–271 in R. Young and L. Norby, editors. Geological Monitoring. Geological Society of America, Boulder, Colorado, USA. http://nature.nps.gov/geology/monitoring/slopes.cfm. Accessed 19 September 2011.

Wilpolt, R. H. and D. W. Marden. 1959. Geology and oil and gas possibilities of Upper Mississippian rocks of southwestern Virginia, southern West Virginia, and eastern Kentucky. Bulletin B 1072-K (1959):587–656. U.S. Geological Survey, Reston, Virginia, USA.

Additional References

This section lists additional references, resources, and web sites that may be of use to resource managers. Web addresses are current as of September 2011.

Geology of National Park Service Areas

National Park Service Geologic Resources Division (Lakewood, Colorado). http://nature.nps.gov/geology/

NPS Geologic Resources Inventory. http://www.nature.nps.gov/geology/inventory/gre_publications.cfm

Harris, A. G., E. Tuttle, and S. D. Tuttle. 2003. Geology of National Parks. Sixth Edition. Kendall/Hunt Publishing Co., Dubuque, Iowa, USA.

Kiver, E. P. and D. V. Harris. 1999. Geology of U.S. parklands. John Wiley and Sons, Inc., New York, New York, USA.

Lillie, R. J. 2005. Parks and Plates: The geology of our national parks, monuments, and seashores. W.W. Norton and Co., New York, New York, USA. [Geared for interpreters].

NPS Geoscientist-in-the-parks (GIP) internship and guest scientist program. http://www.nature.nps.gov/geology/gip/index.cfm

Resource Management/Legislation Documents

NPS 2006 Management Policies (Chapter 4; Natural Resource Management): http://www.nps.gov/policy/mp/policies.html#_Toc157232681

NPS-75: Natural Resource Inventory and Monitoring Guideline: http://www.nature.nps.gov/nps75/nps75.pdf

NPS Natural Resource Management Reference Manual #77: http://www.nature.nps.gov/Rm77/

Geologic Monitoring Manual
R. Young and L. Norby, editors. Geological Monitoring. Geological Society of America, Boulder, Colorado. http://nature.nps.gov/geology/monitoring/index.cfm

NPS Technical Information Center (Denver, repository for technical (TIC) documents): http://etic.nps.gov/

Geological Survey and Society Websites

Kentucky Geological Survey: http://www.uky.edu/KGS/

Tennessee Division of Geology: http://www.tn.gov/environment/tdg/

Virginia Division of Geology and Mineral Resources: http://www.dmme.virginia.gov/divisionmineralresources.shtml

U.S. Geological Survey: http://www.usgs.gov/

Geological Society of America: http://www.geosociety.org/

American Geological Institute: http://www.agiweb.org/

Association of American State Geologists: http://www.stategeologists.org/

Other Geology/Resource Management Tools

Bates, R. L. and J. A. Jackson, editors. American Geological Institute dictionary of geological terms (3rd Edition). Bantam Doubleday Dell Publishing Group, New York.

U.S. Geological Survey National Geologic Map Database (NGMDB): http://ngmdb.usgs.gov/

U.S. Geological Survey Geologic Names Lexicon (GEOLEX; geologic unit nomenclature and summary): http://ngmdb.usgs.gov/Geolex/geolex_home.html

U.S. Geological Survey Geographic Names Information System (GNIS; search for place names and geographic features, and plot them on topographic maps or aerial photos): http://gnis.usgs.gov/

U.S. Geological Survey GeoPDFs (download searchable PDFs of any topographic map in the United States): http://store.usgs.gov (click on “Map Locator”).

U.S. Geological Survey Publications Warehouse (many USGS publications are available online): http://pubs.er.usgs.gov

U.S. Geological Survey, description of physiographic provinces: http://tapestry.usgs.gov/Default.html

Appendix: Scoping Session Participants

The following is a list of participants from the GRI scoping session for Cumberland Gap National Historical Park held on June 6 and 7, 2007. The contact information and email addresses in this appendix may be outdated; please contact the Geologic Resources Division for current information. The scoping meeting summary was used as the foundation for this GRI report. The original scoping summary document is available on the GRI publications web site: http://www.nature.nps.gov/geology/inventory/gre_publications.cfm.

Name	Affiliation	Position	Phone	E-mail
Beeler, Jenny	NPS-CUGA	Natural Resource Specialist	606-246-1113	Jenny_beeler@nps.gov
Connors, Tim	NPS – GRD	Geologist	303-969-2093	Tim_Connors@nps.gov
Crawford, Matt	Kentucky Geological Survey	Geologist	859-257-5500 ext 140	mcrawford@uky.edu
Greb, Stephen	Kentucky Geological Survey	Geologist	859-257-5500 ext. 136	greb@uky.edu
Heller, Matt	Virginia Division of Mineral Resources	Geologist	434-951-6351	Matt.heller@dmme.virginia.gov
Kohl, Martin	Tennessee Division of Geology	Geologist	865-594-5597	Martin.kohl@state.tn.us
Kristovitch, Christine	NPS-CUGA	SCA	606-246-1114	Christine_kristovitch@partner.nps.gov
Martinez, Rodney	NPS-CUGA	Biological Science Technician	606-246-1115	Rodney_martinez@nps.gov
Norby, Lisa	NPS – GRD	Geologist	303-969-2318	Lisa_norby@nps.gov
Overfield, Bethany	Kentucky Geological Survey	Geologist	859-257-5500 ext 132	boverfield@uky.edu
Paylor, Randy	Kentucky Geological Survey	Karst Geologist	859-257-5500 ext 161	rpaylor@uky.edu
Phillips, Christopher	NPS-CUGA	Superintendent's Assistant	606-246-1050	Christopher_phillips@nps.gov
Saltz, AJ	College of William and Mary	SCA	434-665-5381	ajsalt@wm.edu
Taylor, Alfred	Virginia Division of Mineral Resources	Geologist	276-676-5577	Alfred.taylor@dmme.virginia.gov
Teodorski, Scott	NPS-CUGA	Interpreter	606-246-1074	Scott_teodorski@nps.gov
Thornberry-Ehrlich, Trista	Colorado State University	Geologist-Report Writer		tthorn@cnr.colostate.edu
West, Larry	NPS-SER	I&M Coordinator	404-562-3113 ext. 526	Larry_west@nps.gov
Williams, Scott	Virginia Division of Mineral Resources	Geologist	276-623-8276	Scott.williams@dmme.virginia.gov
Woods, Mark	NPS-CUGA	Superintendent	606-246-1052	Mark_woods@nps.gov

NPS 380/10577, September 2011

www.ingramcontent.com/pod-product-compliance
Lightning Source LLC
Chambersburg PA
CBHW081138290526
45795CB00006B/2289

* 9 7 8 1 4 9 1 2 4 7 9 7 6 *